Five Forks

Left: Maj. Gen. George E. Pickett. Library of Congress, Prints and Photographs Division, LC-BH8301-3754.

Right: Maj. Gen. Philip H. Sheridan. U.S. Army Military History Institute, from the collection of the Massachusetts Commandery of the Military Order of the Loyal Legion of the United States.

Five Forks

Waterloo of the Confederacy

A CIVIL WAR NARRATIVE

Robert Alexander

Michigan State University Press • *East Lansing*

∞ The paper used in this publication meets the minimum requirements
of ANSI/NISO Z39.48-1992 (R 1997) (Permanence of Paper).

Michigan State University Press
East Lansing, Michigan 48823-5245
Printed and bound in the United States of America.

09 08 07 06 05 04 03   1 2 3 4 5 6 7 8 9 10

LIBRARY OF CONGRESS CATALOGING-IN-PUBLICATION DATA
Alexander, Robert (Robert E.), 1949–
Five Forks : Waterloo of the Confederacy : a Civil War narrative / by Robert Alexander.
p. cm.
Includes bibliographical references.
ISBN 0-87013-671-2 (casebound : alk. paper)
1. Five Forks, Battle of, Va., 1865—Fiction. 2. United States—
History—Civil War, 1861–1865—Fiction. I. Title.
PS3551.L35744 F58 2003
813.'54—dc21
2002153206

Part of "Calhoun's Monument" first appeared in *The Talking of Hands: Unpublished
Writing by New Rivers Press Authors* (Minneapolis, Minn.: New Rivers Press, 1998).

Every effort has been made to trace copyright holders of quoted material in this book.
The author apologizes if any work has been used without permission and would be
glad to be told of anyone who has not been consulted.

Cover design by Heather Truelove Aiston
Book design/composition by Sharp Des!gns, Lansing, MI

Visit Michigan State University Press on the World Wide Web at *www.msupress.msu.edu*

In memory of

Dorothy Richardson, 1908–2002

who taught me what it means

to have a Southern heart

— Five Forks: At this obscure point, on the afternoon of April 1, 1865, General Philip H. Sheridan launched massive Federal assaults that broke the Southern lines after a nine-month stalemate. Lee's outnumbered army, starving on its feet, then started on a one-hundred-mile "corridor of sorrows" that would end at Appomattox.

— JAMES I. ROBERTSON JR., *Civil War Sites in Virginia*

— Sheridan now began to exhibit those traits that always made him a tower of strength in the presence of an enemy. He put spurs to his horse, and dashed along in front of the line of battle from left to right, shouting words of encouragement, and having something cheery to say to every regiment. "Come on, men," he cried; "go at 'em with a will! Move on at a clean jump, or you'll not catch one of 'em. They're all getting ready to run now, and if you don't get on to them in five minutes they'll every one get away from you! Now go for them!" Just then a man on the skirmish-line was struck in the neck; the blood spurted as if the jugular vein had been cut. "I'm killed!" he cried, and dropped to the ground. "You're not hurt a bit!" cried Sheridan. "Pick up your gun, man, and move right on to the front." Such was the electric effect of his words that the poor fellow snatched up his musket, and rushed forward a dozen paces before he fell, never to rise again.

— HORACE PORTER, *Campaigning with Grant*

RICHMOND TIMES-DISPATCH, SUNDAY, MARCH 24, 1991

Site of Rebel "Waterloo" Is Dedicated

By Jamie C. Ruff
Times-Dispatch state staff

DINWIDDIE—The acquisition of the Five Forks battlefield was praised yesterday as an example of how historic preservation can be achieved through the cooperation of the public and private sectors.

About 100 Tri-Cities civic and political leaders turned out for the dedication of the battlefield, a 930-acre tract five miles north of Dinwiddie Courthouse on state Route 627. The tract is now part of the Petersburg National Battlefield.

Five Forks, named for the roads that intersect there, is known as the Waterloo of the Confederacy. By the time the battle there ended April 1, 1865, Union troops had finally broken the Confederate lines—ending the 10-month siege of Petersburg and cutting the Army of Northern Virginia's last supply line. Within days Gen. Robert E. Lee surrendered at Appomattox.

The battlefield was high on the list of sites the park service wanted to protect.

James W. Coleman, Jr., the park service's regional director, called the battlefield acquisition an example of "our dedication to our rich past" and a sterling example of the concept of the American Battlefield Protection Program, intended to bring private and federal resources together to protect important sites.

The park service was authorized to purchase the tract in 1962, but at the time the landowner, Joseph Peterson Gilliam, did not want to sell. By the time Gilliam was willing to sell, the park service did not have the money.

Eventually, his nephew inherited the land and was receptive to selling the battlefield site. In August 1989 the Conservation Fund of Arlington purchased the tract and on Dec. 29 the land was donated to the park.

"Here at Five Forks, we have shown there is a cost-effective way to protect these sites that made America great," said Edwin C. Bearss, chief historian for the National Park Service.

Acquiring the land was particularly sweet because it is essentially unchanged from the time the battle was fought. The surrounding area is still rural. At the site, except for two houses and an old gas station, the fields look much as they did the day of the battle. The old gas station has been converted into a visitor center and the two houses will be torn down.

There had been three skirmishes in the area over the two previous days when, on March 29, 1865, Lee told Maj. Gen. George E. Pickett to "hold Five Forks at all hazards."

The 10,000 Confederates quickly dug in, but the next day, when Union troops did not attack in mass, the commanders of the Confederate forces, Pickett and Maj. Gen. Fitzhugh Lee, left their troops to join Gen. Thomas Rosser for a shad bake.

Union Maj. Gen. Philip Sheridan attacked at 4:15 P.M. with his 22,000 troops. By the time Pickett learned of the advance and returned, the battle was practically over.

Contents

Preface

THE BATTLE OF FIVE FORKS was fought in a few hours, but this book has taken me more than a decade to complete. In the process, my marriage has dissolved (a "civil war" of a different sort), and I find myself, along with the rest of the planet, embarking on a new century—indeed, as we like to tell ourselves, a new millennium. So this story has the quaintness to me of a period piece, something dressed up in lavender and lace, something you might find up in the attic on a rainy afternoon . . . growing drowsy with the sound of raindrops hitting the roof above you. Or try a different metaphor: it has the look of something receding behind you in the rearview mirror as you glance up, knowing as you do that it's only for a brief moment that you can take your eyes off the highway ahead. Or perhaps the rear seat is packed to the gills with your *stuff* as you move from one city to another, so looking up at the rearview mirror merely gives you a look at your own baggage, and you look to the left and right side-view mirrors instead. There, as you merge back into traffic, you see the message clearly spelled out: OBJECTS IN MIRROR ARE CLOSER THAN THEY APPEAR.

ROBERT ALEXANDER
Madison, Wisconsin
April 1, 2001

Five Forks

I

Springtime
in Virginia

Last Stand of Pickett's Men. Battle of Five Forks. Drawing by Alfred R. Waud, April 1, 1865. Library of Congress, Prints and Photographs Division, LC-USZ62-14304.

I t's springtime now in Virginia and the forsythia is sprouting and the dogwood flowering, splashes of yellow and red and white. There are great expanding buds on the trees, mourning doves lowing in the loblolly pines, cardinals among the cherry blossoms, green magnolias, mists in the dawn . . . and when the sun gets above the trees the pine woods smell warm and sweet. April 1st is cloudless after days of rain. A mockingbird sings in the bright clear morning.

Five Forks could be anywhere, just a country crossroads. It could be anywhere: a fine day out in the woods, with the damp smell of the earth and last year's rotting leaves. It's places like these where war comes—anywhere at all—in the spring countryside with the sound and smell of battle. . . .

—◆—

In graduate school, years ago, a couple of friends and I met once a week at Sonny's to eat pizza and drink red wine and talk about Shakespeare. Across the street the concrete tower of the English department stood motionless as winter ebbed into spring.

One afternoon Gordon talked about the history plays. Gordon had been reading Heidegger, and, so he explained, the histories were a good example of how it is that we meet our past coming to us out of the future. Abe Lincoln, Gordon told us, was an avid reader of Shakespeare's history plays.

In a flash of wine-and-pizza insight, cars gliding by silently beyond the plate glass window, I saw that the soul of Shakespeare's history plays had transmigrated over four centuries into a TV miniseries. And indeed, just as Shakespeare picked his history carefully (he could please or offend the ruling Tudors, depending on how he framed the wars of succession a century or two before his time), I found myself drifting back to the days of Abe Lincoln's presidency—brought to you by Chevrolet, the Heartbeat of America.

— Robert Penn Warren: To begin with, the Civil War offers a gallery of great human images for our contemplation. It affords a dazzling array of figures, noble in proportion yet human, caught out of Time as in a frieze, in stances so profoundly touching or powerfully mythic that they move us in a way no mere consideration of 'historical importance' ever could.[1]

— Edmund Wilson: Has there ever been another historical crisis of the magnitude of 1861–65 in which so many people were articulate? . . .

The drama has already been staged by characters who have written their own parts; and the peculiar fascination of this literature which leads one to go on and on reading it is rather like that of Browning's The Ring and the Book, in which the same story is told from the points of view of nine different persons.[2]

— WALT WHITMAN: The War of Attempted Secession has, of course, been the distinguishing event of my time.[3]

On the small screen of my mind, Union and Confederate generals strut about, declaiming Shakespearean lines as pompously as Mark Twain's Duke and Dauphin. *Night. Another part of the field.* Harry and Hotspur somewhere in Virginia, the spring of 1865. Dim and smoky campfires, councils of war. Harsh glances and savage words: *The Road to Appomattox*, perhaps, a dozen hours of docudrama, a full week of prime-time TV.

From a thespian point of view, all war—despite the vagaries of chance, despite differences in manpower and resources—comes down to an ultimate contest of will between the two commanding generals. On the Southern side stands Robert E. Lee, fifty-eight years old at Appomattox, former superintendent of West Point. Lee was a longtime career soldier in the U.S. Army, who had fought in the Mexican War and whose father, Light Horse Harry Lee, a compatriot of George Washington, had been a cavalry commander in the Revolutionary War. In 1859, while at home on leave in Arlington, Lee was chosen to go take charge of the situation at Harper's Ferry, where some crazy man named John Brown and a bunch of Free-Soilers had taken hostages and were holed up in the federal armory threatening to start a slave rebellion in Virginia.

— WALT WHITMAN: As the period of the war recedes, I am more than ever convinced that it is important for those of us who were on the scene to put our experiences on record.[4]

BALTIMORE, MONDAY, OCTOBER 17, 1859

A dispatch just received here from Frederick, and dated this morning, states that an insurrection has broken out at Harper's Ferry, where an armed band of Abolitionists have full possession of the Government Arsenal. The express train going east was twice fired into, and one of the railroad hands and a negro killed, while they were endeavoring to get the train through the town. The insurrectionists stopped and arrested two men, who had come to town with a load of wheat, and, seizing their wagons, loaded them with rifles, and sent them to Maryland. The insurrectionists number about 250 whites, and are aided by a gang of negroes. At last accounts, fighting was going on.[5]

Lieutenant Colonel Robert E. Lee—aided by Lieutenant Jeb Stuart and a company of U.S. Marines—made quick work of what in fact turned out to be only twenty-some individuals. The survivors, John Brown and six of his followers, were tried, convicted, and hanged for insurrection. Less than two years later, when the war Brown had anticipated broke out in 1861, Lee was offered command of the Federal armies, but declined. Soon thereafter, he resigned his commission and accepted command of the Virginia forces when, following her sister states of the Deep South, Virginia seceded. Four years later, Lee is in command of all the Southern armies.

— WALT WHITMAN: It does not need calling in play the imagination to see that in such a record as this lies folded a perfect poem of the war comprehending all its phases, its passions, the fierce tug of the secessionists, the interminable fibre of the national union, all the special hues & characteristic forms & pictures of the actual battles with colors flying, rifles snapping, cannon thundering, grape whirring, armies struggling, ships at sea or bombarding shore batteries, skirmishes in woods, great pitched battles, & all the profound scenes of individual death, courage, endurance & superbest hardihood, &

splendid muscular wrestle of a newer larger race of human giants with all furious passions aroused on one side, & the sternness of an unalterable determination on the other.[6]

On the Federal side is Ulysses S. Grant, fifteen years younger than Lee. In 1854, Grant had resigned from the army—perhaps in part because of a drinking problem—and later rejoined, a political appointee, at the start of the war. In the interim, after various failed ventures, he had worked in his father's leather store in Galena, Illinois. By 1864, three years into the war, he has become commanding general of the Union armies. A year later, he is on the verge of victory—a good example of how war takes men who seem to have no particular success in civilian life and makes of them illustrious heroes or killers, depending on your point of view.

— WALT WHITMAN: My idea of a book of the time, worthy the time . . . incidents, persons, places, sights . . . a book full enough of mosaic but all fused in one comprehensive theory . . . My idea is a book of handy size and form . . . to cost, including copyright, not more than thirty-five cents or thereabouts to make; to retail for a dollar. I think an edition, elegantly bound, might be pushed off for books for presents, etc., for the holidays, if advertised for that purpose. It would be very appropriate. I think it is a book that would please women. I should expect it to be popular with the trade.[7]

— EDMUND HATCHER: Those who were witnesses and participants in the great struggle can vouch for the correctness of this compilation, while those who have since appeared on the stage may find herein food for the production of an imaginary picture of the closing days of the war, that they will never be able to properly paint.[8]

AMERICA'S BLOODIEST WAR. More American soldiers died in the Civil War than in all the wars of the twentieth century combined. Out of a total population of about thirty million, more than three million soldiers served—half of all military-age males—on both sides of the Mason-Dixon line. Two out of three men wore Federal uniforms (and 10 percent of those were African-American volunteers). All told, there were approximately seven hundred thousand battle casualties, with two hundred thousand deaths. Another four hundred thousand men died of disease or "other causes." Years later, wanderers in the Virginia woods would stumble upon skeletons—soldiers who had crawled away during the heat of battle to die, and who were never found.

In all, more than one million men, one in every three soldiers, was a casualty of the war. Throughout the nineteenth century the American people would bear the scars of the Civil War, and the country would be irrevocably changed. "The past is never dead," William Faulkner said. "It's not even past."

Well over a century after what many still see as the "War to Free the Slaves," one in four black men in their twenties is in prison or on probation or parole—and, not coincidentally, the percentage of total U.S. population in prison is the highest of any nation in the world. Black unemployment is double that of the white working class. And according to the *New York Times*, a man from Harlem has less chance of reaching the age of forty than someone from Bangladesh.

In an economic sense the war was about slavery, as a system of agricultural production in which plantation owners had different interests than the industrialists of the North. But even many abolitionists had no intention of extending to their black neighbors all the "natural" rights expressed by Jefferson in the Declaration of Independence—at least not when it came to living next door and dating *your* daughter—rights enjoyed, to some degree, by all white male Americans.

And there's still no Lincoln automobile dealer in the city of Charleston (though there is in the poorer, racially mixed northern suburbs)—Charleston, the so-called *hotbed of secession,* where in the year or so before the war it could be dangerous to one's personal safety to sound like a fellow who hailed from Boston, the so-called *cradle of abolition.*

— MARY CHESNUT: I remember feeling a nervous dread & horror of this break with so great a power as U.S.A. but I was ready & willing— S.C. had been so rampant for years. She was the torment of herself & everybody else. Nobody could live in this state unless he were a fire eater—come what would I wanted them to fight & stop talking . . . [they] had exasperated & heated themselves into a fever that only bloodletting could ever cure—it was the inevitable remedy. So I was a Seceder—but I dreaded the future. I bore in mind Pugh's letter, his description of what he saw in Mexico when he accompanied an invading Army. My companions had their own thoughts & misgivings doubtless, but they breathed fire & defiance.[9]

By 1860, the year Abe Lincoln is elected president of the "United" States, steam is supplanting horseflesh: railroad mileage in the States has increased fourfold in the decade before the war. The South, however, often by choice, is being left behind as the nation industrializes. Only 20 percent of the nation's railroads lie below the Mason-Dixon line; the broad rivers of the South serve well enough for the shipping of cotton and other agricultural products.

Through birth and immigration, the total U.S. population has just about doubled every twenty years since independence, reaching more than thirty million by 1860. No longer composed only of North and South, the country includes the Northwest as well (or Midwest, as we now refer to it), a new source of political power. The delicate balance of the Senate has been upset.

America's changing. Spiderlike, the railroad is spreading its network of iron across the country. "The cars" move goods and people from city to city at a speed that alarms those used to horse-drawn wagons; crops reach eastern markets in days instead of weeks. The telegraph, moving information even faster, allows nearly instantaneous trading on financial markets (or, in times to come, the manipulation of distant men and armies). The telegraph fosters as well the growth of "national" newspapers, like Horace Greeley's *New York Tribune*. The Associated Press is formed in 1848, and local events like the Lincoln-Douglas debates receive wide coverage.

America's moving into the age of industry. The McCormick reaper, invented by a Virginian from the Shenandoah Valley, enables an expanding population of farmers in the prairie states to compete for world markets. (This machine, doing the work of many laborers, will soon allow a generation of young American farmers to leave their home fields for the battlefield; Grant later calls the reaper his secret weapon.)

America's changing—and the South is hanging back. Factories are sprouting up across the North, and their owners want a tariff levied on imported manufactured goods. But the South remains an agricultural society, and landowners rely for much of their income on the export of King Cotton: they produce, with slave labor, 80 percent of the world's crop. They still import most of their manufactured goods from abroad—and hence, Southerners oppose a tax on imports.

As Bob Dylan would say a century later, "The times they are a-changing."

— WALT WHITMAN: Those hot, sad, wrenching times—the army volunteers, all states, or North or South; the wounded, suffering, dying; the exhausting, sweating summers; marches, battles' carnage; those trenches hurriedly heaped by the corpses, thousands, mainly unknown—will the America of the future, will this vast, rich Union ever realize what itself cost back there, after all? . . . O far-off reader, this whole book is indeed finally but a reminiscent memorial from thence by me to you.[10]

IN THE BEGINNING of April 1861, just weeks after he was inaugurated as president (and four bloody years before Appomattox), Abe Lincoln made a decision not to surrender Fort Sumter to the secessionist government of South Carolina. Instead, he sent ships to resupply its garrison. In so doing, Lincoln provoked the South into firing the first shot—four thousand shots, in fact, before the garrison at Fort Sumter put up the white flag. By then, soldiers had been living through incoming hell for thirty-three hours, and the interior of the structure was on fire—the first modern bombardment in world history.

  ⎯ WALT WHITMAN: The events of '61 amazed everybody north and south, and burst all prophecies and calculations like bubbles. But even then, and during the whole war, the stern fact remains that . . . *the secession cause had numerically just as many sympathizers in the free as in the rebel States.*

  As to slavery, abstractly and practically (its idea, and the determination to establish and expand it, especially in the new territories, the future America) it is too common, I repeat, to identify it exclusively with the south. In fact down to the opening of the war, the whole country had about an equal hand in it. The north had at least been just as guilty, if not more guilty; and the east and west had. The former Presidents and Congresses had been guilty—the governors and legislatures of every northern State had been guilty, and the mayors of New York and other northern cities had all been guilty—their hands were all stain'd.[11]

The day after the flag came down at Fort Sumter, President Lincoln called up seventy-five thousand troops to deal with "combinations too powerful to be suppressed by the ordinary course of judicial proceedings." Four years later to the day—April 15, 1865—Lincoln died of a gunshot wound to the back of his head.

— WALT WHITMAN: Future years will never know the seething hell and the black infernal background of countless minor scenes and interiors (not the official surface-courteousness of the Generals, not the few great battles) of the Secession War; and it is best they should not—the real war will never get in the books. In the mushy influences of current times, too, the fervid atmosphere and typical events of those years are in danger of being totally forgotten. I have at night watch'd by the side of a sick man in the hospital, one who could not live many hours. I have seen his eyes flash and burn as he raised himself and recurr'd to the cruelties on his surrender'd brother, and mutilations of the corpse afterward. . . .

Such was the War. It was not a quadrille in a ball-room. Its interior history will not only never be written—its practicality, minutiae of deeds and passions, will never be even suggested . . . perhaps must not and should not be.[19]

It has been said that the Civil War was the first war fought with modern weapons—rifled artillery firing explosive shells, for example, and by the end of the war, rapid-fire small arms. But tactics remained medieval, involving direct frontal assaults on entrenched positions. It was more often than not a bloodbath.

The first war with modern weapons was also the last to be fought with medieval medicine. Since sterile practice was unheard of and antibiotics nearly a century away, infection of wounds ran rampant. After performing amputations with unclean instruments (reused many times in the chaos of the field hospital), surgeons often moistened their sutures with saliva to assist in threading the needle; consequently the patient's postsurgical course often ran downhill through sepsis to an early death. Morphine had been around since early in the century, but the use of a hypodermic syringe was still a rarity—although, like opium, morphine could be given orally and was often sprinkled into open wounds. (In the latter half of the nineteenth century, drug addiction became known as "old soldier's disease.")

Still, more men died from dysentery—the "Virginia Quickstep"—than from wounds received in battle. Lee himself was reportedly struck with a severe bout of diarrhea the night before ordering General George Pickett's disastrous charge at Gettysburg. Lee was seen, in obvious distress, making repeated trips to the latrine. Does this perhaps explain his lack of judgment in sending Pickett's men to their doom?

Contrary to expectation, it wasn't the pale boys from cities who suffered the most from illness but rather the sturdy lads from the farm. Living at close quarters with primitive sanitation was an unhealthy change from the country. City boys, conversely, had been exposed since childhood to the diseases of group living and therefore had some immunity, plus they thrived on the healthy regimen of sleeping in the open air and getting plenty of exercise. More often it was the farm boys who sickened and died—sometimes, indeed, from "nostalgia," as they called the severe depression that befell men homesick for quieter days and nights.

— WALT WHITMAN: The preceding notes may furnish a few stray glimpses into that life, and into those lurid interiors, never to be fully convey'd to the future . . . the interminable campaigns, the bloody battles, the mighty and cumbrous and green armies, the drafts and bounties—the immense money expenditure, like a heavy-pouring constant rain—with, over the whole land, the last three years of the struggle, an unending, universal mourning-wail of women, parents, orphans—the marrow of the tragedy concentrated in those Army Hospitals (it seem'd sometimes as if the whole interest of the land, North and South, was one vast central hospital, and all the rest of the affair but flanges). . . .

Think how much, and of importance, will be—how much, civic and military, has already been—buried in the grave, in eternal darkness.[13]

2

***

A Cocked
Hat

***

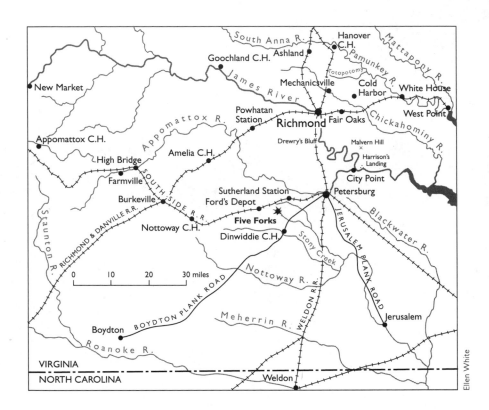

New Market

South Anna R.

Hanover C.H.

Goochland C.H.

Ashland

Pamunkey R.

Mattapony R.

James River

Mechanicsville

Cold Harbor

White House

Appomattox R.

Powhatan Station

Richmond

Fair Oaks

West Point

Chickahominy R.

Appomattox C.H.

High Bridge

Amelia C.H.

Drewry's Bluff

Malvern Hill ×

Harrison's Landing

Farmville

SOUTH SIDE R.R.

Sutherland Station

City Point

Burkeville

RICHMOND & DANVILLE R.R.

Ford's Depot

Petersburg

Staunton R.

Nottoway C.H.

Five Forks

Dinwiddie C.H.

Stony Creek

Blackwater R.

JERUSALEM PLANK ROAD

0   10   20   30 miles

Nottoway R.

WELDON R.R.

Boydton

BOYDTON PLANK ROAD

Meherrin R.

Jerusalem

Roanoke R.

VIRGINIA

NORTH CAROLINA

Weldon

Ellen White

Picture, if you will, the map of Virginia. By 1864, the western counties form a separate state—and Virginia, like a cocked hat, sits astride the South. Toward the hat's peak is the District of Columbia, flower of a nation, just barely out of reach of the Southern army. At the center of the hat of Virginia, where the brain would be in more peaceful times, sits Richmond, Capital of the Confederacy.

IT'S A SHORT DRIVE from Washington to Richmond down I-95, once you get away from the city—across the Potomac, away from the Pentagon and National Airport—and assuming you're going at a time when there's not much traffic, say late morning, perhaps. "Richmond and Points South," the green sign reads over the freeway.

This time of year the hillsides and forests are just beginning to come alive. The woods are already green because of all the pine, but there's a lighter shade of green like mist, and splashes of red and white throughout the forest. The air is warm and slightly humid.

As you leave the city behind, the first mileage signs read "Richmond 90 Miles." An hour and a half. What could be easier?

For fighting conventional battles with conventional armies, Virginia presents the worst sort of terrain. It may be only ninety miles from Washington to Richmond, but the rivers flow west to east—what is it, three, four major rivers between the two cities?—each one together with its tributaries carving a low valley through the piedmont down toward Chesapeake Bay: the Rappahannock, the Rapidan, the Pamunkey, the North Anna. The Federal troops have to cross these rivers, often at this time of year, spring, when they are apt to be at flood stage, leaping out of their banks and taking control of all land within half a mile. And then, as the Unionists try to cross the river, and once they get to the other side, they have to face sixty-five thousand angry Confederate troops under the command of a defensive genius who can usually out-think the opposition by several steps. And the Southern boys know the roads, too, the backwoods clay-and-dirt tracks through tangled forests. And they have modern weapons that have the range on troops from a mile away (when it's possible to see that far through the woods), far enough to give the poor fellow unfortunate enough to be part of a frontal assault something to think about all his remaining days—if he survives this day, that is.

⟶ MARY CHESNUT: When we read of the battles in India, in Italy, in the Crimea—what did we care? Only an interesting topic like any other to look for in the paper.

Now you hear of a battle with a thrill and a shudder. It has come home to us. Half the people that we know in the world are under the enemy's guns.

A telegram comes to you. And you leave it in your lap. You are pale with fright. You handle it, or dread to touch it, as you would a rattlesnake—worse—worse. A snake would only strike you. How many, many, this scrap of paper may tell you, have gone to their death.[1]

Halfway to Richmond, just at the edge of commuting distance to Washington, sits the old river town of Fredericksburg. It's here that in December 1862, commanded by Major General Ambrose Burnside (he of the bald head and thick "sideburns" that carry his name into posterity), Federal troops cross the Rappahannock. They march through town and up a steep hill, Marye's Heights, into the mouths of Confederate muskets and artillery. Confederate troops, behind a stone wall, cut the Federals to bloody pieces while sustaining very few casualties themselves. It's here, witnessing the spectacle of Yankee death and retreat, that Lee reportedly says, "It is well that war is so terrible, otherwise we should grow too fond of it."

⟶ MOXLEY SORREL: In front of us it was hammer and tongs all day from 11 A.M. until finally Burnside had to desist in sheer weariness of slaughter. His troops advanced to their assaults with the finest intrepidity, but it was impossible for them to stand before our fire. I afterwards saw that perhaps not more than half a dozen of their men had got within sixty yards of our wall and dropped there.[2]

This blood-soaked ground was fought over in three successive years: the Battles of Fredericksburg, 1862; Chancellorsville, 1863; the Wilderness and Spotsylvania, 1864. Driving off the interstate, you will pass the strip malls on the edge of town: First Virginia Bank, Century 21 Real Estate, Mr. Donut, Tobacco Bar. Turning off onto a side road, you pass Mary Washington College, a school that used to be the sister school of U.Va., back when Jefferson's university was for white men only.

There's a large open field and a clustered group of buildings to the right; a sign reads, "Mary Washington College Battlefield Athletic Complex and Physical Plant Department." Turning onto an even smaller side road, you drive by a "reconstructed" stone wall, behind which Lee's troops shot the hell out of the Yankees. This is right next to the gift shop and National Cemetery, a steep hillside of graves.

Across from the National Cemetery on Marye's Heights is the Battlefield Cafe. The idea of eating, of grabbing a burger at the place where thousands of men died—this idea nauseates you. You drive on to Richmond.

IN 1864, AFTER THREE years of war, the country faces a stalemate, no clear winner or loser; it seems the war might last forever. "Here was a stand-off," says Grant in his memoirs—but finally, with Grant, the Union has a commander who won't take no for an answer. For this reason, his men call him Butcher. Yet it's said that his dinner meat must be cooked dry, that any trace of blood on his plate sickens him.

No withdrawing back over the Rappahannock for Grant. Previously, when Union commanders had been met by Lee, after a day or two of hard fight they had withdrawn to lick their wounds. No army this size, in this kind of terrain, can get a clear advantage on the other, particularly when the army on the defensive has time to fortify its positions, and the men in it are familiar with the terrain, and they are defending their own territory.

Thus for three years there had occurred inconclusive battle after inconclusive battle, attended by terrible suffering: the woods catching fire from exploding shells, the wounded being burned alive as they tried to crawl away, the smoke, the screams, the stench of burning flesh.

       — ULYSSES S. GRANT: Soon after midnight, May 3d–4th, the Army of the Potomac moved out from its position north of the Rapidan, to start upon that memorable campaign, destined to result in the capture of the Confederate capital and the army defending it. This was not to be accomplished, however, without as desperate fighting as the world has ever witnessed; not to be consummated in a day, a week, a month, or a single season. The losses inflicted, and endured, were destined to be severe; but the armies now confronting each other had already been in deadly conflict for a period of three years, with immense losses in killed, by death from sickness, captured and wounded; and neither had made any real progress toward accomplishing the final end. . . . The campaign now begun was destined to result in heavier losses, to both armies, in a given time, than any previously suffered; but the carnage was to be limited to a single year, and to accomplish all that had been anticipated or desired at the beginning in that time. We had to have hard fighting to achieve this. . . .

The country over which the army had to operate, from the Rapidan to the crossing of the James River, is rather flat, and is cut by numerous streams which make their way to the Chesapeake Bay. The crossing of these streams by the army were generally made not far above tide-water, and where they formed a considerable obstacle to the rapid advance of troops even when the enemy did not appear in opposition. Most of the country is covered with a dense forest, in places, like the Wilderness and along the Chickahominy, almost impenetrable even for infantry except along the roads. . . . The roads were narrow and bad. All the conditions were favorable for defensive operations.[3]

— CHARLES C. COFFIN: The appointment of General Grant to the command of all the armies was not only the beginning of a new *régime*, but the adoption of a new idea—that Lee's army was the objective point, rather than the city of Richmond.

"The power of the Rebellion lies in the Rebel Army," said General Grant to the writer one evening in June last. We had been conversing upon Fort Donelson and Pittsburg Landing. One by one his staff officers dropped off to their own tents, and we were alone. It was a quiet, starlit night. The Lieutenant General was enjoying his fragrant Havana cigar, and was in a mood for conversation, not upon what he was going to do, but upon what had been done. He is always wisely reticent upon the present and future, but agreeably communicative upon what has passed into history.

"I have lost a good many men since the army left the Rapidan, but there was no help for it. The Rebel army must be destroyed before we can put down the Rebellion," he continued.

There was a disposition at that time on the part of the disloyal press of the North to bring General Grant into bad odor. He was called "The Butcher." Even some Republican Congressmen were ready to demand his removal. General Grant alluded to it and said:

"God knows I don't want to see men slaughtered; but we have appealed to arms, and we have got to fight it out."

He had already given public utterance to the expression, "I intend to fight it out on this line, if it takes all summer."

Referring to the successive flank movements which had been made, from the Rapidan to the Wilderness, to Spotsylvania, to the North Anna, to the Chickahominy, to Petersburg, he said:

"My object has been to get between Lee and his southern communications."[4]

— MARY CHESNUT: The dreadful work of death is beginning again.[5]

— WALT WHITMAN: Then the camps of the wounded—O heavens, what scene is this?—is this indeed *humanity*—these butchers' shambles? There are several of them. There they lie, in the largest, in an open space in the woods, from 200 to 300 poor fellows—the groans and screams—the odor of blood, mixed with the fresh scent of the night, the grass, the trees—that slaughter-house! O well it is their mothers, their sisters cannot see them—cannot conceive, and never conceived, these things. One man is shot by a shell, both in the arm and leg—both are amputated—there lie the rejected members. Some have their legs blown off—some bullets through the breast—some indescribably horrid wounds in the face or head, all mutilated, sickening, torn, gouged out—some in the abdomen—some mere boys— many rebels, badly hurt—they take their regular turns with the rest, just the same as any—the surgeons use them just the same. Such is the camp of the wounded—such a fragment, a reflection afar off of the bloody scene—while over all the clear, large moon comes out at times softly, quietly shining.[6]

IN 1864, GRANT, HAVING just turned forty-two, is finally at the helm of the Union Army. After the slaughter at the Battle of the Wilderness, he doesn't withdraw the Army of the Potomac as Hooker did after Chancellorsville, but instead he moves east, trying to get around Lee's flank. But Lee manages to stay ahead of Grant and always keeps his Army of Northern Virginia between Grant and Richmond: the Wilderness, Spotsylvania, Cold Harbor. . . .

— RUFUS DAWES:
May 3rd, 1864.
We move at midnight.

May 11th.
Through God's blessing I am yet alive, and beside the fearful tax upon my energies, mental and physical, have nothing to complain of and everything to be thankful for. For six long days we have been under the deadly musketry. On the morning of May 5th our brigade lost near eight hundred men; the same night a hundred more; the next morning two hundred more.

May 14th.
By the blessing of God I am still alive. We have had continued fighting and hardship since I wrote two days ago, beyond what I can now describe. We charged upon the enemy's rifle pits again on Thursday, and were as usual driven back.

May 15th.
Our army is fearfully exhausted and worn out.

May 16th.
Last night we were ordered to charge the enemy's entrenchments, provided he attacked Burnside's corps on our right, but no attack was made and for the time being we were spared another scene of horrid butchery. We know absolutely nothing of what is going on outside of our army or even within it.

May 17th.

Day after day we stupidly and drearily await the order that summons us to the fearful work.

May 18th.

Alive and well this morning. There has been sharp fighting to our right, indeed there is heavy skirmishing along the whole line as I write.

May 19th.

It is impossible to conjecture when this campaign will end or what will be the result. The country, as usual, has been unduly exultant. This campaign has been by far the most trying I have known. We have had eight days and nights of constant toil and battle.

May 20th.

The battle was on the road to Fredericksburg, directly in our rear. The rebels attacked us. This does not look like Lee was entirely defeated, does it? . . . The enemy are probably reinforced, and I do not believe General Grant will again attack them in their entrenched position.

May 23rd.

Alive, well, south of the North Anna river in the advance of the Fifth Corps. Battle tomorrow—.

May 24th.

I wonder if a man can go forever without being hurt in battle.

May 25th.

We are again closing our lines for a desperate battle. The bullets clip through the green leaves over my head as I lie behind the breastwork writing. I have had no full night's sleep since May 7th, when I took command of the regiment. Day after day, and night after night we have marched, fought and dug entrenchments; I have not changed my clothing since May 3rd.

May 26th.

It is raining steadily. I have a little shelter tent with logs piled up at the end toward the enemy to stop bullets, and I lie on the ground as I write. I presume General Grant will not make an assault upon the enemy in their entrenchments.

May 29th.

Two days and nights of incessant marching has placed us within seventeen miles of Richmond, the heart of the rebellion.

May 31st.

Alive and well. There has been heavy fighting along most of the line.

June 3rd.

We are strongly entrenched and only artillery can harm us. We can not show our heads above the works without being immediately shot at. The men try putting hats on ramrods and sticking them up and sometimes get a bullet through the hat. . . . Thirty-one days today this terrible campaign has dragged along. God grant it soon over.

June 4th.

I can not tell you how tedious and trying this campaign has become. Thirty days of toil, danger and bloodshed, and we can see yet small prospect of an end to it. We are nine miles from Richmond, and our left, by desperate fighting, is said to have been pushed nearer. Our casualties in the regiment now amount to one hundred and seventy men killed and wounded. By general orders we make a daily report of killed and wounded, and we always have some. How long will it take to whittle us away?

June 8th.

We came down here to-day, and are located on the left flank of our army, and we are at last out from under the fire of the enemy. I have enjoyed the luxury of a good wash, a change of clothing, and a *mess of wild strawberries.* It does seem pleasant to get even for a few hours out of the presence of death, suffering and danger. Our spirits rise wonderfully. It is impossible for one who has not undergone it, to fully understand the depression of spirits caused by such long, continued, and bloody fighting and work. Colonel Bragg said yesterday: "Of all I have gone through, I can not now write an intelligent account. I can only tell my wife I am alive and well. I am too stupid for any use." We are having the first quiet day for more than a month. General Cutler said that this is the first day, for that length of time, that no man in the division has been reported killed or wounded. The weather is bright and sunny, and our location is delightful.

June 9th.

All is quiet with us here. We can plainly see the enemy south of the Chickahominy. Our pickets are friendly, and we get the morning papers from Richmond by 10 o'clock in the forenoon.

June 16th.

We have a rumor that General Hancock has taken Petersburg. If he has not it will cost us a bloody battle.

June 19th.

Yesterday afternoon in another hopeless assault there was enacted a horrid massacre of our Corps. Our brigade charged half a mile over an open field, under the musketry fire of the enemy.

June 21st.

The suicidal manner in which we are sent against the enemy's entrenchments is discouraging. Our brigade was simply food for powder in the assault day before yesterday.

June 22nd.

Still skulking in our holes, and dirty, dusty places they are, but the Johnnies leave us no alternative.

June 25th.

Imagine a hole three feet wide and four feet deep in the middle of the street, and a sun perfectly sweltering in its rays and you have our quarters, from which we can not raise our heads.

July 2nd.
There is an ice house on our skirmish line. I have some boys who have the nerve to go out and get the ice at night, in spite of the fact that rebel sharpshooters keep a constant fire on the ice house. There is one good thing, Corps headquarters can't put a guard over it, and gobble it away from us, and appropriate it to their own use.

July 5th.
To the right of us Burnside's negroes occupy the trenches. Master and slave meet on equal terms and the hostility is implacable. They fire night and day on both sides.

July 10th.
We are in the trenches again, but the rebel infantry is very friendly. A villainous shell occasionally shrieks over our heads, but does no further harm than to create a kind of shivering sensation that "the Angel of Death has spread his wings on the blast."

July 13th.
I am myself the only man who has passed unharmed through every battle and skirmish of the regiment.

July 17th.
There is now no mortar or artillery firing along the line. Before today the enemy would throw a mortar shell into our lines at intervals of about fifteen minutes.

July 22nd.
I strolled along our line of entrenchments today. It would seem that our army is impregnably entrenched.

July 30th.
Our men gained the enemy's works and took their line, and the position

held would have broken the rebel army. But victory stands with the enemy, who drove our men out and regained all they had lost.

August 1st.

We are today about four miles from the enemy and upon the extreme left of the army. It seems comfortable to get almost out of hearing of the shooting. I have put the regiment into camp and I have fixed up a fine and shady bower for my headquarters. Day before yesterday's failure will likely make summer bowers fashionable for this army.

August 5th.

The weather is very hot and things go on with the usual stale monotony of a summer life in camp. Occasionally we hear a burst of cannon and mortars in the distance, but we are out of the way of them. We have orders to get under arms at daylight every morning.

September 1st.

It seems almost certain to me that I could never have lived through another such carnival of blood. Only eighty men are left in the ranks for service.[7]

FINALLY GRANT SLIDES EAST and south and ends up below Richmond, crossing the James River on June 15, trying to get at Lee from Petersburg, a small town twenty miles from Richmond with immense strategic significance because it's the hub of four rail lines. But by the time Grant crosses the James, he is too late to trap Lee—the Confederate lines are intact all the way to Petersburg and beyond.

The summer drags on, a summer of immense heat and drought. General Phil Sheridan with the cavalry has been sent to lay waste to the rich cropland of the Shenandoah Valley. The two armies settle down to trench warfare. From the time the Union Army crossed the Rappahannock, at the beginning of May, until the pause in fighting at the end of June, the Federals lost more troops than Lee's entire army contained at the start of the campaign. But the Union has seemingly inexhaustible resources, and new men and supplies keep coming. The veteran troops complain about the quality of "bounty men" and paid-for substitutes they see showing up in camp—but unlike the Army of Northern Virginia, the Federal troops do get reinforcements. Horses get fed and shod, uniforms are replaced when they wear out.

 ALEXANDER GARDNER: The parched ground and arid appearance of the landscape was characteristic of the country about Petersburg, where the constant movements of troops crushed out vegetation. Forests, houses, and fences were swept away, and the fields were transformed into vast commons, where the winds raised clouds of sand, and covered everything with the sacred soil. On these glaring deserts, with no covering but the shelter tent and withered brush, the army toiled and fought through many months, filling the valleys with graves, and sapping the vigor of men in the prime of life. . . .

Excavations were made in the ground, and covered first with heavy pieces of timber, over which a layer of earth, of several feet in thickness, is thrown, sufficient to resist the penetration and explosion of any shell that might fall upon them. The interior of these habitations were made as comfortable as possible. . . . The scene presents a singular and grotesque appearance—to be appreciated it must be seen; no description will prove adequate. Few know the hardships and discomforts through which soldiers have to pass.[8]

Fifty years later, there will be a Great War that again leads to trench warfare and murderous assaults against unbreachable positions—slaughters that will make Gettysburg look like a playground scuffle. But for the next half century, from the Civil War to the Great War, the images arising from Petersburg represent to the rest of the world the horrors of trench warfare. The American Civil War was the first war to be recorded by photographs: single walls left standing, windows empty against the sky, the rest of the building destroyed by artillery fire—and on the battlefield, rows of corpses.

⟶ MARY CHESNUT: Now this horrible vision of the dead on the battlefield haunts me.[9]

Sometimes after the two armies had been fighting for days, the commanding generals had to call a limited armistice so the bodies could get buried, the smell was so bad. In the Virginia summer heat, the merciless sun, flesh rotted quickly.

⟶ WILLIAM CLARK CORSON: Our cavalry is encamped all around here in the driest, hottest, poorest and altogether the meanest country between the mountains and tide water. The dust is everywhere from six inches to knee deep and the slightest breeze blows it about in clouds reminding one of the descriptions given by travelers of a storm upon the desert of the Sahara. Water is exceedingly scarce. . . .

The horses in camp are living on a retrospective view of the past and the hope of a better day coming. For several days after we got in our horses got nothing. They are now allowing them about a bundle of oats a day and a few handfuls of corn. . . .

The enemy still throw shells into Petersburg and burn a few houses every day. A portion of the city is entirely deserted. The Yankees can destroy the city at any time they wish. . . .

Not a drop of rain for six weeks and vegetation dying rapidly.[10]

IT'S LATE SUMMER NOW. In the early evening the leaves of the pin oak in the back-yard move imperceptibly in the faint breeze off the water. And it's hot. Lying in the hammock in the shade of the huge tree, I feel as if I can barely breathe.

In the distance the sporadic rumble of artillery, pounding away. A house in the next block was hit yesterday—pretty fairly demolished, it was. But next to it there's a house with only one wall gone. It's like a stage set—looking at the furniture, looking into someone else's life. Was anyone home at the time?

Probably not, since most everyone's left this part of the city by now. There's still plenty of food, though, put up by folks and then abandoned as they fled before the invaders. Though to be sure the invaders haven't actually got here yet. Just their "hot shot and shell."

In the hot fading summer twilight the breeze picks up slightly off the water. In the distance I can hear the crash and rumble of artillery at the outskirts of town. My dog cowers as she does in a thunderstorm, though it hasn't rained for two weeks. The top leaves of the pin oak move delicately against the sky.

THE SIEGE OF PETERSBURG contains many elements of modern warfare: the ruined structures of a ruined city, men in trenches living with mud and vermin and disease, the immense constructions of wood and dirt that continue for mile after mile, the constant shelling, the snipers. The winter, when it finally arrives that year, is unbelievably cold. The Confederates in their trenches, who lack both food and warm clothes, have a miserable time of it. The saying goes around that it's "a rich man's war and a poor man's fight."

Only in retrospect does anyone find it romantic.

↣ CONSTANCE CARY HARRISON *(from a letter she received):* "Lord! Lord! What a dazzling, wholesome high-bred little society it was. Night after night, I galloped into town to attend dances, charades, what not? and did not get back to my camp until two—three—what matter the hour?—but was always up, fresh as paint, when the reveillé bugles blew, and when, a little later on, my first sergeants reported to me as adjutant with their Battery Reports.

"To you and me, looking back, it was such a blending of a real 'Heroic Age' and a real 'Golden Age' as could come but once in a million years. Everybody knew everybody (in the highest sense of that phrase), and there was youth, and beauty, and devotion, and splendid daring, a jealous honor and an antique patriotism, an utter self-abnegation and utter defiance of fate, a knightly chastity and beautiful surrender (of the coyest maiden when her lover was going to certain death). God! what a splendid high society that little handful was! Oh! I never talk of it now. People would only say, 'Why, there wasn't one of them worth $100,000.'"[11]

↣ HENRY ALEXANDER WHITE: Winter poured down its snows and its sleets upon Lee's shelterless men in the trenches. Some of them burrowed into the earth. Most of them shivered over the feeble fires, kept burning along the lines. . . . Most of them were clad in mere rags. Gaunt famine oppressed them every hour.[12]

Now it's spring again, 1865. At City Point, just southeast of Petersburg, the *River Queen* rests at her mooring. The old river steamer has been pressed into military use, and in the captain's boardroom, Abraham Lincoln is meeting with his officers. It's cool tonight, at the end of March. Occasionally the boat creaks. (A year later, after the war ends, the *River Queen*, back in private hands, will be used to host a party at the annual New York Yacht Club Regatta.)

At Grant's invitation, Lincoln has come down from Washington to get a firsthand look at the situation closer to the front, and talk to his commanders: Grant, Sherman, Admiral Porter. The president hopes the war is nearly over, the killing done. He asks, "Do you think things might be resolved without more bloodshed?" Grant replies that he thinks not, he thinks it might take one final great battle.

On Good Friday, barely two weeks later—five days after Lee surrenders to Grant at Appomattox—Lincoln will be shot at Ford's Theater, and lie dying all night.

All about the *River Queen* rest a multitude of ships; during the day City Point is a scene of nearly indescribable bustle and energy, a focal point for the overwhelming resources the Federal government has devoted to the war. But at night, all is quiet here at the confluence of the James and Appomattox Rivers. The *River Queen* might just as well be alone in the hostile, silent Virginia darkness.

⟶ John Gibbon: To me, Mr. Lincoln wore an exceedingly haggard and careworn expression and seemed to be filled with anxiety in regard to the coming struggle which all could see could not be postponed now many days. . . . His great, gaunt, ungainly form was always a welcome sight to the soldiers and I think he was the homeliest man I ever saw, especially when he *laughed.* I rode beside him on horseback as he left the review ground and could not help noticing his silent abstracted manner and sad careworn face.[13]

⟶ Abraham Lincoln: I could not have been long in bed when I fell into a slumber, for I was weary. I soon began to dream. There seemed to be a death-like stillness about me. Then I heard subdued sobs, as if a number of people were weeping. I thought I left my bed and wandered downstairs. There the silence was broken by the same pitiful sobbing, but the mourners were invisible. I went from room to room; no living person was in sight, but the same mournful sounds of distress met me as I passed along. It was light in all the rooms; every object was familiar to me; but where were all the people who were grieving as if their hearts would break? I was puzzled and alarmed. What could be the meaning of all this? Determined to find the cause of a state of things so mysterious and so shocking, I kept on until I arrived at the East Room, which I entered. There I met with a sickening surprise. Before me was a catafalque, on which rested a corpse wrapped in funeral vestments. Around it were stationed soldiers who were acting as guards; and there was a throng of people, some gazing mournfully upon the corpse, whose face was covered, others weeping pitifully. "Who is dead in the White House"' I demanded of one of the soldiers. "The President," was his answer; "he was killed by an assassin!"[14]

It's spring now, the roads are drying out, and Grant wants to get Lee out in the open for one last decisive battle. Of course, Grant has been wanting to do that for a year or so, and it's not been so easy to accomplish. He figures if he can get around Lee's right—where the Confederate lines are getting stretched thinner and thinner—Lee will have no choice: abandon Richmond and Petersburg, and meet the far more numerous Federals without benefit of fortifications, or get trapped. But Grant's fear is that Lee will escape before the Union troops can get around his flank. Moving south to Carolina by the Richmond and Danville Railroad, Lee could then hook up with Joe Johnston and fall on Sherman with the two combined armies. Then, having defeated Sherman, they could together turn on Grant.

— Ulysses S. Grant: I was afraid, every morning, that I would awake from my sleep to hear that Lee had gone, and that nothing was left but a picket line.[15]

— Andrew A. Humphreys: The country was flat, covered generally with dense forest and tangled undergrowth, with numerous small, swampy streams, that, owing to the flatness of the country, did not drain the downfall quickly. The soil was a mixture of clay and sand, partaking in some places of the nature of quicksand.[16]

— Ulysses S. Grant: Sometimes a horse or mule would be standing apparently on firm ground, when all at once one foot would sink, and as he commenced scrambling to catch himself all his feet would sink and he would have to be drawn by hand out of the quicksands so common in that part of Virginia and other southern States.[17]

— Charles C. Coffin: The work which General Grant had in hand was the seizure of the South Side Railroad by an extension of his left flank. . . .

To comprehend the movement, it is necessary to understand the geographical and topographical features of the country, which are somewhat peculiar. Hatcher's Run is a branch of the Nottoway River, which has its rise in a swamp about four miles from the Appomattox and twenty southwest of Petersburg. The South Side Railroad runs southwest from Petersburg, along the ridge of land between the Appomattox and the headwaters of the Nottoway, protected by the swamp of Hatcher's Run and by the swamp of Stony Creek, another tributary of the Nottoway.

The point aimed at by General Grant is known as the "Five Forks," a place where five roads meet, on the table-land between the head-waters of Hatcher's Run and Stony Creek. It was the most accessible gateway leading to the railroad. If he could break through at that point, he would turn Lee's flank, deprive him of the protection of the swamps, use them for his own cover, and seize the railroad. To take the Five Forks is to take all; for the long and terrible conflict had become so shorn of its outside proportions, so reduced to simple elements, that, if Lee lost that position, all was lost—Petersburg, Richmond, his army, and the Confederacy. . . .

Lee's line of retreat must necessarily be towards Danville; but Grant, at the Five Forks, would be nearer Danville by several miles than Lee; and he would thus, instead of the exterior line, have the interior, with the power to push Lee at every step farther from his direct line of retreat.[18]

— PHIL SHERIDAN: I tell you, I'm ready to strike out tomorrow and go to smashing things.[19]

ONE LINE OF ESCAPE for Lee, the South Side Railroad, goes west from Petersburg, crossing the Danville Road about forty miles from the city, at Burkeville, and proceeding to Lynchburg and the Blue Ridge. Lee's army could by this route escape to the mountains. But what Grant and Sheridan have in mind will forestall this: get around in front of Lee as he retreats west from Petersburg, cut the Danville Road, his escape route south, and the South Side Railroad, his escape route west. Trap Lee between the James and the Appomattox. Like a bottle, the area between the two rivers narrows about a hundred miles west of Petersburg. If Sheridan can get the cavalry around in front of Lee, and if the Fifth Corps infantry can move fast enough to support Sheridan, they will trap Lee's whole army. At the mouth of the bottle sits a small town, Appomattox. If the Federals can move fast enough, that's where they will finish Lee off.

— PHILIP CHEEK: March 27th we could hear skirmishing on the left. On March 28th had brigade inspection and received orders to be ready to move at 3 A.M. tomorrow. In the afternoon we played ball.[20]

TELEGRAM

Cavalry Headquarters,
March 31, 1865.
Lieut. Gen. U. S. Grant,
Commanding Armies of the United States:

General: My scouts report the enemy busy all last night in constructing breastworks at Five Forks, and as far as one mile west of that point. There was great activity on the railroad; trains all going west. . . .

P. H. Sheridan, Major-General.[21]

So speed is most important, to keep Bobby Lee from slipping the noose. As soon as the roads dry out from the spring rains, it will be too late. Lee will vanish as he has so many times before. Got to get started NOW. You can't let him get the jump on you (like a runner stealing second). Get Sheridan with his cavalry around Lee's right, around past Burgess' Mill and Dinwiddie Court House. Get Lee out in the open, where we can really have at him!

HARPER'S MONTHLY (MAY 1865)

But Grant had determined that the evacuation of Manassas should not be repeated here—that the retreat of Lee's army from Richmond should not proceed deliberately to its conclusion, and at its own motion. He forthwith assumed the offensive. Sheridan's cavalry was now beginning to come up. Giving this 'rough rider' scarcely time to newly shoe his horses, Grant hurried him off toward Dinwiddie Court House, with the Fifth Corps moving on the right as an infantry support.[22]

➤ ULYSSES S. GRANT: My hope was that Sheridan would be able to carry Five Forks, get on the enemy's right flank and rear, and force them to weaken their center to protect their right so that an assault in the center might be successfully made.[23]

➤ WALT WHITMAN: Few realize how sharp and bloody those closing battles were. Our men exposed themselves more than usual; press'd ahead, without urging. Then the southerners fought with extra desperation. Both sides knew that with the successful chasing of the rebel cabal from Richmond, the game was up. The dead and wounded were unusually many.[24]

➤ WALTER TAYLOR: On the first day of April General Grant directed a heavy movement against the Confederate right near Five Forks; this necessitated the concentration of every available man at that point to resist the Federal advance, and a consequent stretching out of our line, already so sadly attenuated that at some places it consisted of but one man to every seven yards—nothing more than a skirmish line.[25]

⟶ MORRIS SCHAFF: As soon as Lee, in the course of the forenoon of April 1st, Saturday, heard that Sheridan was likely to renew the offensive, he started several brigades under Anderson to Pickett's help . . . but before Anderson could reach Pickett, Sheridan, reinforced by Warren, assailed him and drove him with great confusion from the field, capturing thousands of prisoners and several guns, the uncaptured Confederates fleeing northward in utter confusion through the darkness, for it was just at nightfall that they met their overwhelming defeat.[26]

TELEGRAM

Headquarters Army of Northern Virginia,
April 1, 1865.
Hon. Secretary of War.
Richmond, Va.

Sir: After my dispatch of last night I received a report from General Pickett, who, with three of his own brigades and two of General Johnson's, supported the cavalry under General Fitz Lee near Five Forks, on the road from Dinwiddie Court House to the South Side Road. After considerable difficulty, and meeting resistance from the enemy at all points, General Pickett forced his way to within less than a mile of Dinwiddie Court House. By this time it was too dark for further operations, and General Pickett resolved to return to Five Forks to protect his communication with the railroad. He inflicted considerable damage upon the enemy and took some prisoners. His own loss was severe, including a good many officers. . . .

General Pickett did not retire from the vicinity of Dinwiddie Court House until early this morning, when, his left flank being threatened by a heavy force, he withdrew to Five Forks, where he took position with General W. H. F. Lee on his right, Fitz Lee and Rosser on his left, with Roberts' brigade on the White Oak road connecting with General Anderson. The enemy attacked General Roberts with a large force of cavalry, and after being once repulsed finally drove him back across Hatcher's Run. A large force of infantry, believed to be the Fifth Corps, with other troops, turned General Pickett's left and drove him back on the White Oak road, separating him from General Fitz Lee, who was compelled to fall back across Hatcher's Run. General Pickett's present position is not known. . . .

> Very respectfully, your obedient servant,
> R. E. Lee, General.[27]

— Morris Schaff: Pickett's and Fitz Lee's failure to hold that position was fatal, and offered a singular instance of Fortune's bad turn of her wheel for Lee; inasmuch as, when Sheridan made his attack, the famous, long-haired Pickett, Gettysburg's hero, and the cavalry commanders, blue- and gay-eyed Fitz Lee, gigantic, high-shouldered and black-eyed Rosser, were engaged in planking shad on the north bank of Hatcher's Run, two miles or more in the rear of their resolute but greatly outnumbered troops. Although the fire was quick and heavy, it was completely smothered by the intervening timber, and notwithstanding the heroic efforts of the gallant Munford and the infantry brigade commanders, before Fitz Lee, Pickett and Rosser got to the front the day was lost; so at least the story was told to me by my friend Rosser, who lately and in honor went to his grave.[28]

George Pickett, Virginian, infantry commander at Five Forks, had been appointed to West Point, class of 1846, at the suggestion of an older friend from Illinois (where Pickett's uncle lived)—a small-town lawyer named Abe Lincoln. Pickett ended up graduating last among fifty-five classmates. And Robert E. Lee's nephew, Fitzhugh Lee, another

Virginian, is Pickett's cavalry commander at Five Forks. (Thirty-some years later, Fitz Lee will be major general of American volunteers during the Spanish-American War, leading the invasion of Cuba if not in fact the actual charge up Kettle Hill—North and South reunited in a still-segregated U.S. Army.)

By Sunday, April 2, the war is nearly over: the Confederate defeat the afternoon before at Five Forks has sealed the doom of Lee's army.

With nearly five thousand Confederates captured by the Federal troops—the loss of most of Pickett's command, though the cavalry escaped to fight again—Lee is forced to abandon Richmond and Petersburg the next day, another balmy spring day by all accounts. Since Lee has fewer than fifty thousand troops altogether, and Grant has more than twice that number, the Confederate math comes up short: at this point there are no more than a thousand soldiers available for each mile of fortifications—far less than one soldier per yard, the rule of thumb taught at West Point as the minimum number for a successful siege defense.

— CAPTAIN ROBERT E. LEE JR.: On April 1st the Battle of Five Forks was fought, where about fifty thousand infantry and cavalry—more men than were in our entire army—attacked our extreme right and turned it, so that, to save our communications, we had to abandon our lines at Petersburg, giving up that city and Richmond.[29]

Jefferson Davis gets Lee's message to evacuate Richmond while he's at morning services in St. Paul's Episcopal Church, and the service deteriorates to a hubbub as everyone realizes what's happening. One week later and a hundred miles to the west, Lee will surrender to Grant at Appomattox.

— THOMAS T. MUNFORD: It was at the battle of Five Forks, on the evening of April 1st, 1865, that the sun of the Southern Confederacy went down and the star of its destiny set. . . . It was but a battle on a small scale: compared with such struggles of armies as Malvern Hill, Sharpsburg, Second Manassas or Gettysburg, it could be classified as a mere skirmish. But no other fight of the entire four years war was followed by such important consequences. It was the immediate cause of the flight of President Jefferson Davis from Richmond; it compelled General R. E. Lee to evacuate the old fortifications he had held so long and against such tremendous odds, before he was ready to do so; it forced his retreat towards Appomattox. It extinguished the campfires of the hitherto invincible army and was the mortal wound which caused the Southern Confederacy to perish forever.[10]

As COMMANDING OFFICER at the shad bake, Major General George Pickett earned Robert E. Lee's special and continuing ire. Several days later, Lee will ask, "Is that man still in the army?" But even before the battle of Five Forks, Lee and Pickett dislike each other, each one perhaps blaming the other for the defeat at Gettysburg. In his letters to his future wife, Pickett refers to Lee as the "Great Tyee," which in Tlingit (Pickett was stationed near Vancouver Island before the war) means King Salmon— or, colloquially, Big Fish.

After the war, Lee is said to snub Pickett one afternoon at the Spotswood Hotel; Pickett then turns to his companion, John Mosby, and says, "That old man murdered my boys." At Gettysburg, two-thirds of the men in Pickett's division died or were wounded or went missing in their ill-fated attack on Cemetery Ridge.

— SPENCER GLASGOW WELCH: On the third day the fighting began early in the morning and continued with the greatest imaginable fury all day; at one time, about three o'clock in the afternoon, with such a cannonading I never heard before. About 150 pieces of cannon on our side and as many or more on the side of the enemy kept up one incessant fire for several hours. It was truly terrifying and was like heavy skirmishing in the rapidity with which the volleys succeeded one another. The roar of the artillery, the rattle of the musketry and the wild terrific scream of the shells as they whizzed through the air was really the most appalling situation that could possibly be produced.[31]

— JAMES LONGSTREET: I asked the strength of the column. [Lee] stated fifteen thousand. Opinion was then expressed that the fifteen thousand men who could make successful assault over that field had never been arrayed for battle; but he was impatient of listening, and tired of talking, and nothing was left but to proceed.[32]

— GEORGE PICKETT: "Great God," said Old Peter as I came up. "Look, General Lee, at the insurmountable difficulties between our line and that of the Yankees—the steep hills, the tiers of artillery, the fences, the heavy skirmish line—and then we'll have to fight our infantry against their batteries. Look at the ground we'll have to charge over, nearly a mile of that open ground there under the rain of their canister and shrapnel."

"The enemy is there, General Longstreet, and I am going to strike him," said Marse Robert in his firm, quiet, determined voice.[33]

— JAMES LONGSTREET: Pickett, I am being crucified at the thought of the sacrifice of life which this attack will make. I have instructed Alexander to watch the effect of our fire upon the enemy, and when it begins to tell he must take the responsibility and give you your orders, for I can't.[34]

— GEORGE PICKETT: I have ridden up to report to Old Peter. I shall give him this letter to mail to you and a package to give you if—Oh, my darling, do you feel the love of my heart, the prayer, as I write that fatal word?[35]

— WALTER HARRISON: The enemy again opened fresh batteries, at short range, which had been reserved for this moment, and their infantry from behind their sheltered position poured a destructive fire of musketry right into the faces of the men as they rushed up to their breastworks.[36]

— JOSHUA L. CHAMBERLAIN: Plowed through by booming shot; torn by ragged bursts of shell; riddled by blasts of whistling canister; straight ahead to the guns hidden in their own smoke; straight on to the red, scorching flame of the muzzles, the giant grains of cannon-powder beating, burning, sizzling into the cheek; then in upon them!—pistol to rifle-shot, saber to bayonet, musket-butt to handspike and rammer; the brief frenzy of passion; the wild "hurrah!" then the sudden, unearthly silence; the ghastly scene; the shadow of death.[37]

According to one eyewitness, Franklin Sawyer of the Eighth Ohio Volunteers, when the Yankee artillery started to fire from Cemetery Ridge, you could hear a collective sigh of anguish rise from the field where Pickett's men marched forward—as flesh and blood dissolved into "a dense cloud of . . . arms, heads, blankets, guns and knapsacks." All that night, you could hear the cries and moans of the wounded.

⟶ FRANK HASKELL: The stricken horses were numerous, and the dead and wounded men lay about, and as we passed these latter, their low piteous call for water would invariably come to us, if they had yet any voice left. I found canteens of water near—no difficult matter where a battle has been—and held them to livid lips, and even in the faintness of death, the eagerness to drink told of their terrible torture of thirst.[38]

⟶ GEORGE PICKETT: Ah, if I had only had my other two brigades a different story would have been flashed to the world.[39]

⟶ ROBERT E. LEE: The loss of our gallant officers and men throughout the army causes me to weep tears of blood and to wish that I could never hear the sound of a gun again.[40]

⟶ MOXLEY SORREL: Every brigade commander and colonel and lieutenant colonel of Pickett's division was shot down.[41]

It was James Longstreet who espoused a theory of defensive warfare, having seen firsthand at Marye's Heights what entrenched forces could do to advancing infantry. That's why he told Lee at Gettysburg, before Pickett's charge, that no fifteen thousand troops in the history of the world could take the Yankee position: uphill a mile or more against artillery and entrenched infantry. But after the war Longstreet became the scapegoat for the Confederate loss at Gettysburg, because on the second day of the battle, the day before Pickett's Charge, he didn't get his troops up in time to take Little Round Top while it was still undefended. In point of fact, Longstreet didn't want to attack at all, which perhaps explains his case of "the slows." The Federals, or so he thought, had the high ground.

Old Pete, as Longstreet was called, tried to convince Lee that the Army of Northern Virginia could accomplish more by trying another tack. What Longstreet wanted was to slip around the Federal left flank, slide on by the Round Tops, and move into the rear of the Yankee army. Having interposed between the Federal troops and Washington, Lee could then find a strong position from which the Union Army would have to dislodge him. The Confederates in this case would have the entrenchments, and the Federals would have to mount a frontal assault.

But Lee felt that to withdraw would be tantamount to retreating, and he would have none of that, despite the fact that his troops at Gettysburg had essentially blundered into contact with the Yankees. Jeb Stuart and the cavalry—Lee's "eyes and ears"—were away on a raid, circling the Army of the Potomac, as they had also done with a lot of bravado a year previously. In this case, however, Lee's army was in Pennsylvania, and his infantry commanders had no idea what they were getting into. Lacking the resourceful Stonewall Jackson, who had died just two months earlier, the Confederates stumbled into the crossroads town of Gettysburg looking for a rumored supply of shoes. But once there, in a deadly tête-à-tête with the Union forces, Lee felt he couldn't back down. *There the enemy is, and there I will attack him.*

Seventy-five years later, in 1938—just one year before a war in which the world would witness the first use of the atomic bomb—there took place at Gettysburg the "last reunion of Blue and Gray." A photograph from that event shows old geezers with canes shaking hands across a stone wall where three-quarters of a century earlier they had tried their damnedest to kill each other.

The electric light. The telephone. Automobiles. The airplane. These veterans had lived to see the rise of industry, the age of the machine. Perhaps they sat around at that last reunion, reminiscing, drinking (as late at night and as much as a fellow in his nineties could manage), listening to someone play J. M. Carmichael's "Long Ago" on the guitar: "Though we are agèd and gray, Comrades, and trials of life are nearly done, / To us life's as dear as it was, Comrades, when you and I were young."

— MOXLEY SORREL: A singular figure indeed! A medium-sized, well-built man, straight, erect, and in well-fitting uniform, an elegant riding whip in hand, [Pickett's] appearance was distinguished and striking. But the head, the hair were extraordinary. Long ringlets flowed loosely over his shoulders, trimmed and highly perfumed; his beard likewise was curling and giving out the scents of Araby.[42]

— FRANK HASKELL: None on that crest now need be told that *the enemy is advancing*. Every eye could see his legions, an overwhelming, resistless tide of an ocean of armed men, sweeping upon us! . . . The first line at short interval is followed by a second, and that a third succeeds; and columns between support the lines. More than half a mile their front extends—more than a thousand yards the dull gray masses deploy, man touching man, rank pressing rank, and line supporting line. Their red flags wave; their horsemen gallop up and down; the arms of eighteen thousand men, barrel and bayonet, gleam in the sun, a sloping forest of flashing steel. Right on they move, as with one soul, in perfect order, without impediment of ditch, or wall, or stream, over ridge and slope, through orchard, and meadow, and cornfield, magnificent, grim, irresistible.[43]

— FRANCIS DAWSON: That sad night not more than three hundred men remained to us of what had been one of the finest divisions in the service. The remnants of the companies were commanded by corporals and sergeants; regiments by lieutenants; and a brigade by a major. Never had Virginia suffered a heavier blow. The division was composed of the flower of her children, and there was weeping and desolation in every part of the Old Dominion.[44]

3

The Fighting
Has Just Begun

Two of Sheridan's Scouts (Sketched from Life by Winslow Homer). Century Illustrated Monthly Magazine 35 (November 1887): 132.

The fluorescent lighting and climate-controlled hiss of the air-conditioning surround me as I sit with the Virginia Historical Society library's century-old magazines. The war, I'm beginning to realize, was fought and refought year after year, in print or over a couple of drinks, as long as two veterans survived to argue about what had really happened and why. "The war is over," they said, "but the fighting has just begun." These voices speak to me from the pages of Confederate Veteran *and the* Southern Historical Society Papers. *This spring morning, the peace and light of the library and the comforting hiss of the air conditioner are a long way from battle.*

THE SMITH PREMIER TYPEWRITER: Leads them all. Elegant, durable. Light and easy touch.

PACIFIC COAST LIMITED: Equipment brand new. Finest trains on wheels. Fastest schedule through the sunny South to sunny California.

SOUTHERN RAILWAYS, the Great Highway of Travel: Reaching the principal cities of the South with its own lines and penetrating all parts of the country with its connections, offers to the traveler unexcelled train service, elegant equipment, fast time.

A REUNIFIED COUNTRY: No North, No South, No East, No West. National Reunion of the Blue and Gray. War dramas, prize drills, military maneuvering, and patriotic speeches will be accompanied by marching soldiers, beating of drums, rattle of musketry, and booming of cannon. This will awaken the martial spirit and bring back to the veteran the impulse of youth.[1]

— CHARLES K. MOSER: In the spring of 1908, while I was an editorial writer on the *Washington Post*, through the recommendation of Colonel John S. Mosby, late guerrilla leader of the Confederacy, or perhaps through his son, John S. Mosby, Jr., I received the manuscript attached hereto entitled "Five Forks: The Waterloo of the Confederacy, or the Last Days of Fitz Lee's Cavalry Division," from General Thomas T. Munford, late cavalry leader of the Confederate

Army. . . . He wished me to put it into shape for submittal to publishers as a book or magazine serial.

We had an exchange of correspondence, all of which has since been lost or destroyed. I rewrote the manuscript, using essentially and wherever possible General Munford's exact language, except in certain instances where it seemed to me impolitic. The MS was then sent to General Munford for examination, and he returned it with his approval and some few interlineations in his own handwriting. . . .

I sent the MS to Mr. Leonard Derbyshire, Publisher and Editor of *The Sunday Magazine*, a syndicated magazine published simultaneously in several hundred newspapers throughout the country. Before decision was made as to its suitability for publication, however, General Munford wrote me asking that publication be held up indefinitely. He had discussed it with his friend, Rev. Dr. Randolph McKim, Rector of the Church of the Epiphany at Washington, D.C., and others of his old comrades-in-arms, who felt that publication while some of the actors in the final scenes of the Confederacy still lived would cause needless distress.

Soon afterward I entered the service of the Department of State, was sent abroad, and never heard from General Munford afterwards. He had, however, left this manuscript with me to do with as I wished (to the best of my recollection) after his death. He was concerned only, he said, with vindication of his old comrades-in-arms of Fitz Lee's Cavalry Division, and with the truth of history.[2]

LATE THAT AFTERNOON I take my dog for a walk across the street from my fiancée's house on the north side of Richmond. There's an undeveloped patch of land in the noise-shadow of the freeway—a rocky creek bed that's usually a trickle but after rain can get to be a shoulder-high torrent in places: ravined sides, granite boulders exposed above the waterline. A couple of huge loblolly pines, an enormous willow oak. Honeysuckle. My dog, beginning to show her years, has trouble getting across the boulders. This creek is nameless on the maps I have of Richmond. I imagine that this is what Hatcher's Run looked like, one spring afternoon 125 years ago, when George Pickett and some other men had a picnic that might have hastened the demise of the Confederacy.

After she gets home from work, my fiancée takes me on a home-buying tour of the city, including for comparison's sake the newest cookie-cutter neighborhoods on the northwest side of the city, far beyond where the outer fortifications protected Richmond from the invading Yankee hordes. Richmond is booming this year; it's the "New South." (I suspect it's been the New South since shortly after the end of Reconstruction.) Metropolitan Richmond has nearly doubled in size in the quarter century since the Civil War centennial.

We start by driving out Monument Avenue, looking at the statues: Stuart, Lee, Davis, Jackson. Some of the statues face north, some south. "The ones who died in the war face north," my fiancée tells me. Protecting Southern soil. "You know," she says, "I had a teacher in high school who still called it the 'late unpleasantness.'"

It's a far cry indeed from Boston, where as a kid going downtown for my cello lessons, my mother driving, we would pass by the William Lloyd Garrison statue on the Common: his abolitionist arm outstretched rhetorically, as some poet has said, to catch pigeon shit. And I remember the equestrian statue of Fighting Joe Hooker on the Statehouse grounds: Hooker, the Union general beaten at Chancellorsville, whose name supposedly has come down to posterity as a tribute to the industrious women who followed his army.

I grew up thinking the Civil War was fought to free the slaves. In grade-school music class we sang "Follow the Drinking Gourd" (a song about following the Big Dipper northward to freedom) and the "Battle Hymn of the Republic" *(Let us die to make men free)*. One of my best friends lived in a house that had a hidden staircase used in the days of the Underground Railroad. I grew up believing in the righteousness of the war.

In a scene from Francis Ford Coppola's film about Vietnam, *Apocalypse Now,* a squadron of Air Cavalry helicopters attacks a Viet Cong position, while Wagner's "Ride of the Valkyries" blasts out of loudspeakers mounted on the outside of the colonel's helicopter. Whether fact or fiction, this scene echoes the Civil War. Sheridan, I've read, had as many as half a dozen brass bands on the field at once. To the crackle and spit of gunfire and the bass thump of artillery, sitting their horses just back of the line of fire, the bands played on: fife and bugle, rotary-valve horns of all sizes, snare drum: "The Army of the Free," "New York Volunteer" (more soldiers came from New York than any other state), "We Are Coming Father Abraham," "The Battle Hymn of the Republic."

While studying the Civil War in eighth grade, my class took a trip south to visit battlefields. It's Centennial time; the last surviving C.W. vet had died a few years back. Our class visits Gettysburg, and I stand on Cemetery Ridge and imagine Pickett's men spread out in the valley before me, battle flags flying, sunlight glinting off the brass of muskets and officers' swords—an immensely impressive line of men *walking* up the long gentle slope, soon to be gentle no longer.

Each student that year had to memorize a portion of *John Brown's Body* and recite it to the class. I chose Pickett's charge: "He had gone out with fifteen thousand. He came back to his lines with five." (When I get to Richmond years later, I visit the Confederate Museum and mention *John Brown's Body* to the cashier in the gift shop. "Yankee trash," the woman said.)

When I had to write a paper, that eighth-grade year, I chose to discuss the success of Sheridan's campaign in the Shenandoah Valley. If I had grown up white in a Southern school, I think that instead of the "Battle Hymn of the Republic," I would perhaps have been singing Innes Randolph's "Good Old Rebel": "Three hundred thousand Yankees is stiff in Southern dust, / We got three hundred thousand before they conquered us." And it would have been the brilliance of Stonewall Jackson's Valley campaign that I would have written about in school.

"Why is it that men are so fascinated by war?" she asks, looking directly at me, her winter-pale face framed by dark hair. She has stopped the car by an old redbrick colonial whose lawn slopes downward toward the James River, which is hidden by thick trees and brush. "I thought you knew," I reply. "You went to Mary Washington College, and walked to class over ground where men bled to death. And besides," I say, "*I'm* not fascinated by war—not like that guy from Quantico you used to date."

(The Quantico Marine Base is just a few miles from the Mary Washington campus, and I've heard, on more than one occasion, of a lieutenant who wrote letters from Vietnam that the censors cut large portions out of, letters about Zippo cigarette lighters and thatch-roofed huts. Now he's practicing law in Miami Beach.)

But there *is* something in the spectacle of a "civil" war that's morbidly fascinating, to be sure: these guys all speak the same language (more or less), have the same George Washington to name their public schools after, salute (until now) the same flag. What's gotten into them, anyway? Many of the generals know each other from West Point (at any given time there were usually fewer than two hundred cadets in residence), and from fighting together in Mexico (America's war of "manifest destiny"). Longstreet, for example, was best man at Grant's wedding.

Both sides have the same songs, though often with slightly different words. Sometimes, for a brief respite of peace, they even sing them together: *a mist hangs over the still river while there rises, from either side, the melancholy strains of Amazing Grace.*

Coffee is rare and expensive in the blockaded South, and Confederate soldiers often trade tobacco to the Yanks for coffee and sugar, at one point using model boats to send supplies back and forth across the Rappahannock—until the officers put a stop to such "fraternizing." If the men get too friendly, after all—as they may if left to their own devices—perhaps they'll no longer be willing to kill each other. When rousted by their officers, the men warn each other: "Two minutes, Reb, then we have to start firing." "Okay, Yank, two minutes, then your ass is grass."

— George E. Smith: All that day, until about four o'clock, the picket-firing was intense, but was abruptly ended by a Confederate challenging a 6th Wisconsin man to a fist-fight in the middle of the turnpike. The combatants got the attention of both picket lines, who declared the fight "a draw." They ended the matter with a coffee and tobacco trade and an agreement to do no more firing at picket lines, unless an advance was ordered.[3]

CHORUS

The Union forever,
Hurrah, boys, Hurrah!
Down with the traitor,
Up with the star;
While we rally 'round the flag, boys,
Rally once again,
Shouting the battle cry of Freedom.

Our Dixie forever,
She's never at a loss,
Down with the eagle,
Up with the cross.
We'll rally 'round the bonnie flag,
We'll rally once again.
Shout, shout the battle cry of Freedom.[4]

IN MY MIND THIS COULD easily be the antebellum Spotswood Hotel: the long table with linen tablecloth, set with crystal and silver, the clinking of silver on china. Evening is slipping into night on the cobblestones outside. The traffic has slowed. It grows quiet in the mahogany-paneled room.

My soon-to-be father-in-law is sitting opposite us. A short energetic man with gray brush-cut hair and thick mustache, to me he will always be the Colonel. For many years he worked for the Department of Defense (which used to be more forthrightly called the Department of War). Shortly after I met him, the Colonel told me, "I've been at meetings in the basement of the Pentagon, in a room with six-inch-thick lead walls." Unthinking, I asked, "What did you talk about there?" "One can't say," he replied.

"Don't say 'Civil War,'" he tells me now. "Say, 'the War between the States.' What an absurd expression, 'Civil War.'

"Let me tell you a story," he says.

It's Europe, the last winter of World War II. Things are slow on that part of the front. One day the Colonel then a mere corporal—receives a gift from his father, a large bottle of maraschino cherries. What the hell, he thinks, I don't even like maraschino cherries, what's he doing, sending me a quart bottle? So these cherries sit around unopened until one afternoon when the Corporal gets hungry. For some reason there's nothing else handy to eat, so he opens the bottle of cherries.

What he finds, to his delight, is that his father has poured off the heavy syrup the cherries were originally packed in, and replaced it with bourbon. "Just sitting there popping the cherries," the Colonel tells me, "you could get a really nice buzz on."

He says, "There were four of us in the squad, manning an antitank gun. We were rotated every twenty-four hours, one team came up and the other went back to town. This was just south of the Battle of the Bulge: like a quarterback shift, we'd been moved up to cover the fellows who went in. It was my day off, but one of the other team was sick, so the lieutenant asked me to stay on. We heard the firefight moving up the valley below us, all the way into town. You know," he says, looking at me, "those other fellows, the four of them, who went to town . . . they were captured. Never heard from again.

"A fellow I met years later, at a meeting, was also captured there—a musician. He told me he threw away his dog tags with the Star of David on them. Word came down they were shooting prisoners, and he managed to escape. He's never talked about it, still couldn't tell me what went down, even after forty years.

"It's funny how that happens," the Colonel says. "I was volunteered to stay on that day. The others were never heard from again."

As the Colonel informs me, fewer than half of all Southerners actually owned any slaves, and many white Southerners were, like Robert E. Lee, opposed to the Peculiar Institution. Fearing the consequences of immediate abolition, however, they envisioned a gradual approach which would provide compensation to the slaveholders for their financial loss. Indeed, the Colonel says, many Americans, both North and South, claimed at the time to be fighting primarily about the right of the Southern states to secede from the Union. In town after town across the North, he adds, you will find monuments from the nineteenth century which give thanks to those who died in the cause of Union—but there is no mention of slavery.

> — HERBERT SAUNDERS: On the subject of slavery, [Lee] assured me that he had always been in favour of the emancipation of the negroes and that in Virginia the feeling had been strongly inclining in the same direction, till the ill-judged enthusiasm (amounting to rancour) of the abolitionists in the North had turned the Southern tide of feeling in the other direction. In Virginia, about thirty years ago, an ordinance for the emancipation of the slaves had been rejected by only a small majority, and every one fully expected at the next convention it would have been carried, but for the above cause. He went on to say that there was scarcely a Virginian now who was not glad that the subject had been definitely settled, though nearly all regretted that they had not been wise enough to do it themselves during the first year of the war.[5]

The Colonel tells me, perhaps too quickly, that the war wasn't fought for slavery. Lincoln called for troops in 1861 to suppress a rebellion, to keep the Southern states within the Union. Yet from the white Southern point of view, it was a "War of Northern Aggression": the States had a *right* to withdraw from a membership that they had voluntarily joined in the first place—as members of a club might do, it was said—and the North was wrong to oppose this by force.

— WALTER HARRISON: A morbid appetite, insatiate with acquisition of new territory, and pugnacious definement of boundary lines, could no longer be appeased by foreign imbroglio, but must needs turn a gluttonous maw upon its own vitals.[6]

— THOMAS JEFFERSON: We, the General Assembly of Virginia, on behalf, and in the name of the people thereof, do declare as follows: The States in North America which confederated to establish their independence of the government of Great Britain, of which Virginia was one, became, on that acquisition, free and independent States, and as such, authorized to constitute governments, each for itself, in such form as it thought best.

They entered into a compact (which is called the Constitution of the United States of America), by which they agreed to unite in a single government as to their relations with each other, and with foreign nations, and as to certain other articles particularly specified. They retained at the same time, each to itself, the other rights of independent government, comprehending mainly their domestic interests. . . .

But the federal branch has assumed in some cases, and claimed in others, a right of enlarging its own powers by constructions, inferences, and indefinite deductions from those directly given, which this assembly does declare to be usurpations of the powers retained to the independent branches, mere interpolations into the compact, and direct infractions of it. . . .

Whilst the General Assembly thus declares the rights retained by the States, rights which they have never yielded, and which this State will never voluntarily yield, they do not mean to raise the banner of disaffection, or of separation from their sister States, co-parties with themselves to this compact. They know and value too highly the blessings of their Union as to foreign nations and questions arising among themselves, to consider every infraction as to be met by actual resistance. They respect too affectionately the opinions of those possessing the same rights under the same instrument, to make every difference of construction a ground of immediate rupture. They would, indeed, consider such a rupture as among the greatest calamities which could befall them; but not the greatest. There is yet one greater, submission to a government of unlimited powers. It is only when the hope of avoiding this shall become absolutely desperate, that further forbearance could not be indulged.[7]

— ROBERT E. LEE: All that the South has ever desired was that the Union, as established by our forefathers, should be preserved, and that the government as originally organized should be administered in purity and truth.[8]

From this point of view, Lincoln and the federal government had claimed for themselves powers they had no constitutional right to—in those hot times *tyranny* and *despotism* were the words Southerners often used. Though he was imprisoned for two years after the war, Jefferson Davis was never put on trial for treason—and some people suspected that perhaps the leaders of the Federal government were afraid the South's constitutional right to secede might be vindicated in court. As white Southerners will tell you, the war was fought, with few exceptions, on Southern soil. It was Southern property that was burned, Southern railroads torn up, Southern farms trampled and destroyed. The Federal troops were invaders, and—as friendly folks will tell you—Southerners fought to protect their homeland.

Finally the Colonel says to me, "There's nothing like the sight of someone trying to kill you to make you pick up your gun and fire back."

AFTER DESSERT AND COFFEE, I consider the irony of paying for dinner with cash. Here we are, I think, in the Capital of the Confederacy, passing paper money that carries Grant's face on it.

In fact, the greenback is another legacy of the Civil War. At first Lincoln thought the idea of these paper certificates somehow fraudulent, since each one would carry a *reproduced* signature as legal tender, but his Treasury secretary, Salmon P. Chase (with presidential ambitions of his own), talked Lincoln into it as the most expedient—not to say essential—way of waging war. *Print all the money you need.* "Immediate action is of great importance," Chase told Lincoln, "the Treasury is nearly empty." (During the Civil War, for the first time, the U.S. national debt surpassed one billion dollars—a significant milestone, to be sure.)

To support the government's ability to repay its war bonds, Congress passed the Internal Revenue Act, taxing goods such as tobacco, liquor, luxury items and patent medicines, putting in place a corporate tax on interest and dividends, a value-added tax on manufactured goods, an inheritance tax—and the first U.S. income tax. For enforcement purposes, the law also created the Bureau of Internal Revenue. Since Lincoln in effect therefore was the father of the modern IRS, it seems somehow appropriate that Americans honor the day of his death, April 15, by sending in their annual tax returns.

One more remnant of the Civil War is the phrase *unconditional surrender.* So I was told by a political scientist from the Library of Congress, Warren Tsuneishi, who sat next to me on the flight from my home in Wisconsin down to Washington. Caught up in travel's anonymity, we shared desultory small talk—but when I mentioned I was researching the Civil War, my seatmate immediately spoke up.

He told me that he had, while in graduate school, tried to find the origin of the term *unconditional surrender,* and though he researched long and hard, he hadn't been able to find any instance of its use before General U. S. Grant demanded it of his old West Point buddy Simon Bolivar Buckner, the Confederate commander at Fort Donelson, Tennessee—the first of Grant's important victories, in the winter of 1862.

"Unconditional Surrender" Grant, he was subsequently called because of the coincidence of his initials—a coincidence that itself resulted from a mix-up when Grant first enrolled at West Point. The name given him at birth was Hiram Ulysses Grant, but because Grant's registered West Point name was Ulysses S. Grant (his mother's maiden name was Simpson), his fellow cadets saw in his first two initials an opportunity too good to pass up. So it was that "Uncle Sam" Grant became, to a North eager for victory, an avatar of the total defeat Union supporters wished upon their enemies.

The Federal government came out of the Civil War immensely more powerful than at its start. In essence, the Confederacy was overwhelmed by the manpower and resources of the (remaining) United States, and the power that Lincoln helped amass in order to ensure victory has remained an essential element of national government.

The value of paper greenbacks on the New York money market was a good barometer of how well Federal forces were doing. At the time of Lee's invasion of Pennsylvania, shortly before Gettysburg, the value of the greenback dropped significantly—there was an increase in the so-called "gold premium"—but the paper dollar rebounded after Lee's defeat. (The rumor was that traders in New York heard the news before it reached the president.)

— JEREMIAH BEST: Paper-money brought every one into Wall Street, and interested every family in the ups and downs of stocks. It circulated like fertilizing dew throughout the land, generating enterprise, facilitating industry, developing international trade. . . .

Within a few weeks after the first issue of legal tenders, stocks began to rise, and rose steadily, with slight interruptions, till April, 1864, when Mr. Chase, by selling his surplus gold for legal tenders, created an unexpected money panic, and the whole fabric of stock speculation toppled to the earth, overwhelming in the ruin thousands of unlucky operators. . . .

In 1863, and in the first quarter of 1864, everybody seemed to be speculating in stocks. Nothing else was talked of at clubs, in the streets, at the theaters, in drawing-rooms. Ladies privately pledged their diamonds as margin with brokers, and astonished their husbands with the display of their gains. Clergymen staked their salary, and some of them realized in a few months more than they could have made by a lifetime of preaching. One man, who had nothing in the world but a horse, sent him to a broker's stable, and persuaded the broker to buy him a hundred shares; he drew from the broker, a few months after, a balance of $300,000.[9]

A year after the Crash of 1864, the war is nearly over. Lee will soon be trapped. The market price of greenbacks is just about at par.

— ROBERT E. LEE: The movement of General Grant to Dinwiddie Court House seriously threatens our position, and diminishes our ability to maintain our present lines in front of Richmond and Petersburg. . . . From this point I fear he can readily cut both the South Side & the Danville Railroads being far superior to us in cavalry. This in my opinion obliges us to prepare for the necessity of evacuating our position on James River at once.[10]

In one of his wartime newspaper columns, Karl Marx explains why—aside from the moral issue of slavery—the Union couldn't live with a separate Confederacy. With control of the Mississippi lost, many Northern farmers had no way to get their crops to market (the railroads weren't up to the task), so Southerners had the Midwest at their economic mercy. Lincoln himself uses this same reasoning in a message to Congress proposing a constitutional amendment for compensated emancipation—and explaining why the North must persevere in its struggle to preserve the Union.

Industrial New England, despite abolitionism, could perhaps have tolerated a separate South to trade with. After all, New Englanders themselves had pioneered the slave trade in North America, and had for economic reasons considered seceding from the Union barely half a century earlier. Just as money could supersede religion any day but Sunday, so could ideology rise to the support of whatever happened to be in *your* best interest.

— E. P. Whipple: The North is fighting for power which is its due, because it is just and right; the South is fighting for independence, in order to remove all checks on its purpose to oppress and enslave.[11]

— Edward Everett Hale: And the issue of this war is the issue between democracy and oligarchy.[12]

There were those who said that some Republican abolitionists were motivated less by humanitarian principles than by their desire for another source of cheap labor for their textile mills. And unlike Southern slaveholders, for whom the slave represented a significant capital investment, the factory owners had no need to provide for the medical care and other domestic needs of their workers.

— Dr. Josiah C. Curtis: There is not a state's prison or house of correction in New England where the hours of labor are so long, the hours for meals so short, and the ventilation so much neglected as in the cotton mills with which I am acquainted.[13]

⚊ ORESTES BROWNSON: Wages is a cunning device of the devil, for the benefit of tender consciences, who would retain all the advantages of the slave system, without the expense, trouble, and odium of being slave-holders.[14]

⚊ LYDIA MARIA CHILD: What can we do with the slaves? is a foolish question. "Take them away from Mr. Lash and place them with Mr. Cash" solves that imaginary difficulty.[15]

In some way it's still a case of Roundhead versus Cavalier—a conflict between the descendants of those who came to America in the seventeenth century instead of staying to fight it out in England. Two centuries later the conflict resumes between New England industrialists and Southern landowners. Slavery, after all, is what has enabled the landed gentry to maintain their feudal agricultural economy an extra century or two. But it's also a case now of Pioneer versus Planter: the rapidly expanding population of the frontier states, together with the old Northeast, outnumbers by more than two to one the Southern planters and townsfolk—and their black "property."

WISCONSIN MEETS VIRGINIA ON FIELD OF BATTLE. Virginia: first of the original thirteen colonies, where black people came ashore at Jamestown in 1619, just a dozen years after the settlement began. And Wisconsin: the last state in the Northwest Territory, where slavery was forever banned, thanks to a slave-owning Virginian, Thomas Jefferson, who wrote the Northwest Ordinance. The Republican Party, the party of abolition, rose from flat Wisconsin farmland.

⚊ ALEXIS DE TOCQUEVILLE: It is easy to perceive that the South, which has given four Presidents to the Union, which perceives that it is losing its federal influence and that the number of its representatives in

Congress is diminishing from year to year, while those of the Northern and Western states are increasing, the South, which is peopled with ardent and irascible men, is becoming more and more irritated and alarmed. Its inhabitants reflect upon their present position and remember their past influence, with the melancholy uneasiness of men who suspect oppression.[16]

COLUMBUS (GEORGIA) SENTINEL, JANUARY 23, 1851

There is a feud between the North and the South which may be smothered but never overcome. They are at issue upon principles as dear and lasting as life itself. Reason as we may, or humbug as we choose, there is no denying the fact that the institutions of the South are the cause of this sectional controversy, and never until these institutions are destroyed, or there is an end to the opposition of the North to their existence, can there be any lasting and genuine settlement between the parties.[17]

— JOHN C. CALHOUN: We of the South will not, cannot surrender our institutions. To maintain the existing relations between the two races, inhabiting that section of the Union, is indispensable to the peace and happiness of both. It cannot be subverted without drenching the country in blood, and extirpating one or the other of the races. Be it good or bad, it has grown up with our society and institutions, and is so interwoven with them, that to destroy it would be to destroy us as a people. But let me not be understood as admitting, even by implication, that the existing relations between the two races in the slaveholding States is an evil:—far otherwise; I hold it to be a good, as it has thus far proved itself to be to both, and will continue to prove so if not disturbed by the fell spirit of abolition. . . .

There is and always has been in an advanced stage of wealth and civilization, a conflict between labor and capital. The condition of society in the South exempts us from the disorders and dangers resulting from this conflict; and which explains why it is that the political condition of the slaveholding States has been so much more stable and quiet than that of the North. The advantages of the former, in this respect, will become more and more manifest if left undisturbed by interference from without, as the country advances in wealth and numbers. We have, in fact, but just entered that condition of society where the strength and durability of our political institutions are to be tested.[18]

⏤ WILLIAM H. SEWARD: In the field of federal politics, Slavery, deriving unlooked-for advantages from commercial changes, and energies unforeseen from the facilities of combination between members of the slaveholding class and between that class and other property classes, early rallied, and has at length made a stand, not merely to retain its original defensive position, but to extend its sway throughout the whole Union. . . .

The plan of operation is this: by continued appliances of patronage and threats of disunion, they will keep a majority favorable to these designs in the Senate, where each State has an equal representation. Through that majority they will defeat, as they best can, the admission of free States and secure the admission of slave States. Under the protection of the Judiciary, they will, on the principle of the Dred Scott case, carry Slavery into all the Territories of the United States now existing and hereafter to be organized.[19]

⏤ SCHUYLER COLFAX: The character of the Code of pretended Laws enacted by the bogus Territorial Legislature of Kansas—a Legislature notoriously forced upon the people of that Territory, at the hands of invading ruffians from Missouri, using the persuasive arguments of the Bowie-Knife and Revolver—may be judged from the following extracts, which are taken from Executive Document No. 23, submitted to Congress by the President of the United States, and printed by the public printer to Congress. The Document forms a volume of 822 pages, and is entitled "Laws of the Territory of Kansas."

CHAPTER 151.—SLAVES

An Act to Punish Offences against Slave Property.

Sec. 3: If any free person shall, by speaking, writing, or printing, advise, persuade, or induce any slaves to rebel, conspire against, or murder any citizen of this territory, or shall bring into, print, write, publish or circulate, or cause to be brought into, printed, written, published or circulated, or shall knowingly aid or assist in the bringing into, printing, writing, publishing, or circulating in this Territory, any book, paper, magazine, pamphlet, or circular, for the purpose of exciting insurrection, rebellion, revolt, or conspiracy on the part of the slaves, free negroes, or mulattoes, against the citizens of the Territory or any part of them, such person shall be guilty of felony, and shall suffer death.[20]

IN THE LONG RUN, of course, both in financial and human terms, it would have been far cheaper for North and South to empower the Federal government to purchase emancipation for all four million slaves. At a thousand dollars per person (an approximate average at the time), this would have amounted to four billion dollars total—and the Federal government could have issued long-term bonds to cover the cost. The war itself would prove far more expensive. (In 1880 the U.S. Treasury reported the cost of the war as six billion dollars, a figure that would nearly double in the next few decades with the cost of veterans' pensions.) But the antebellum Federal government was unable to shoulder that kind of burden: it would take Lincoln and his wartime presidency to bring about deficit spending of that magnitude.

Using just this sort of fiscal logic—that is, the cost balance of continuing the war as opposed to purchasing freedom for all slaves—President Lincoln proposed a constitutional amendment for compensated emancipation, sent to Congress on December 1, 1862, just one month before the Emancipation Proclamation itself took effect. This proposal, generally ignored by history, was the velvet glove around the iron fist of the executive order. Moreover, the Emancipation Proclamation freed slaves only within the belligerent areas. It wasn't until 1865 that the Thirteenth Amendment was passed—without mention of compensation—outlawing the existence of slavery "except as a punishment for crime."

— ABRAHAM LINCOLN: I will say, then, that I am not, nor have ever been, in favor of bringing about in any way the social and political equality of the white and black races; that I am not, nor have ever been, in favor of making voters or jurors of Negroes, nor of qualifying them to hold office, nor to intermarry with white people; and I will say, in addition to this, that there is a physical difference between the white and black races which I believe will forever forbid the two races living together on terms of social and political equality. And inasmuch as they cannot so live, while they do remain together there must be the position of superior and inferior, and I as much as any other man am in favor of having the superior position assigned to the white race.[21]

Most white people felt at the time of the Civil War that the two races could never live together—and so, Southerners wondered before the war, what would happen if there *was* emancipation? African-Americans composed nearly half of the Southern population of nine million, and the grim experience of white planters in Haiti at the turn of the century— killed or exiled after a successful black revolt—encouraged Southerners' fear of what might happen to them at the hands of their own slaves, should matters ever get out of control.

In 1831, a vision-crazed preacher in Southside Virginia by the name of Nat Turner led a half dozen followers on a two-day orgy of violence in which they killed some fifty white people—men, women, and children. White Southerners at that point began to resemble more than ever the fellow who says, looking over his shoulder, "Just remember, even paranoids have enemies." (Two decades later, John Brown would prove this statement true.) This fear resulted in the growth of local militias to contain the perceived threat from black folks and abolitionists—paramilitary units that would later become part of the Confederate Army.

There were some people, both black and white, who felt that a return of African-Americans to Africa, or settlement elsewhere, was the only possible solution—though this too would have entailed huge costs and human disruption. In that same 1862 message to Congress concerning emancipation, Lincoln indicated that he had already proposed to several Latin American countries negotiations on the topic of resettlement.

HARPER'S MONTHLY (JANUARY 1863)

Several of the Spanish-American Republics have protested against the scheme of sending colonies of colored emigrants to their territories, and the President has declined to move any such colony to any State without having first obtained the consent of its Government, and a guarantee that the emigrants should be received and treated as freemen.[22]

As white Southerners would find out after the war, slavery was by no means essential for them to maintain local control, both economic and political. Sharecropping became in some ways even more profitable for landowners than slavery had been, since they were no longer obligated to support those too young, old, or sick to work. Those same planters were not, however, so sanguine before the war, and they feared enormous social repercussions, at the expense of their own ruling class, if their slaves attained their freedom.

    — CHARLES O'CONOR: Our negro bondmen can neither be exterminated nor transported to Africa. They are too numerous for either process, and either, if practicable, would involve a violation of humanity. If they were emancipated, they would relapse into barbarism, or a set of negro States would arise in our midst, possessing political equality, and entitled to social equality. The division of parties would soon make the negro members a powerful body in Congress—would place some of them in high political stations and occasionally let one into the Executive chair.

    It is in vain to say that this could be endured; it is simply impossible.

    What then remains to be discussed?[23]

On no terms at all would most white Southerners have agreed to live as equals with their black neighbors—but in this they were not particularly sectional in nature, as they were joined in prejudice by their countrymen, North or East or West. To be sure, white Northerners and Southerners alike, shipowners and planters, beginning in the early years of the colonies and continuing for two centuries afterward, had conspired in the slave trade. Their sins landed on the heads of their descendants, who would engage in fratricidal conflict to resolve a conflict that could—but for racism, perhaps—have been solved by reason alone.

— NATHANIEL HAWTHORNE: There is an historical circumstance, known to few, that connects the children of the Puritans with these Africans of Virginia, in a very singular way. They are our brethren, as being lineal descendants from the Mayflower, the fated womb of which, in her first voyage, sent forth a brook of Pilgrims upon Plymouth Rock, and, in a subsequent one, spawned slaves upon the Southern soil—a monstrous birth, but one with which we have an instinctive sense of kindred, and so are stirred by an irresistible impulse to attempt their rescue, even at the cost of blood and ruin."[24]

THOUGH MANY HOURS have passed since dinner, it's still dusky gray here in the upstairs bedroom. The curtains are drawn on the dormer windows, and outside there's a full moon shining through the thick loblolly pines. We can see its light dimly here in the bed where I lie beneath you, the ceiling fan turning above your head like a slowly moving halo. The sweat runs from your breasts. The torrents of spring, *I think as I lick a salty drop from your nipple. Your body strains against me. I raise my head to see your face, eyes nearly closed, your head slightly tilted as you look down at me, watching me.*

Like it or not, the dirty little secret of racism is sexual in nature: the desire we feel for the Other, the drive to mingle our DNA and increase the genetic stability of the next generation. It's an explosive mixture. According to the law of the land, the black woman is the master's *possession*, to do with as he will—and, conversely, a black man can be strung up for merely looking longingly at a white woman. And there's more, a horror of biblical proportions: a slaveholder could, of course, sell his own children.

— MARY CHESNUT: I wonder if it be a sin to think slavery a curse to any land. Sumner said not one word of this hated institution which is not true. . . . God forgive us, but ours is a *monstrous* system and wrong and iniquity. Perhaps the rest of the world is as bad—this *only* I see. Like the patriarchs of old our men live all in one house with their wives and their concubines, and the mulattoes one sees in every family exactly resemble the white children—and every lady tells you who is the father of all the mulatto children in everybody's household, but those in her own she seems to think drop from the clouds, or pretends so to think.[25]

— FITZ-HUGH LUDLOW: The record of any one American who has grown up in the nurture of Abolitionism has but little value by itself considered; but as a representative experience, capable of explaining all enthusiasms for liberty which have created "fanatics" and martyrs in our time, let me recall how I myself came to hate Slavery. . . .

Just after the John Brown raid, I went to Florida. I remained in the State from the first of January till the first week of the May following. I found there the climate of Utopia, the scenery of Paradise, and the social system of Hell. . . .

The most open relations of concubinage existed between white chevaliers and black servants in the town of Jacksonville. I was not surprised at the fact, but was surprised at its openness. The particular friend of one family belonging to the cream of Florida society was a gentleman in thriving business who had for his mistress the waiting-maid of the daughters. He used to sit composedly with the young ladies of an evening—one of them playing on the piano to him, the other smiling upon him over a bouquet—while the woman he had afflicted with the burdens, without giving her the blessings, of marriage, came in curtsying humbly with a tea-tray. Everybody understood the relation perfectly; but not even the pious shrugged their shoulders or seemed to care.[26]

— JAMES HENRY HAMMOND: In my last will I made and left to you, over and above my other children, Sally Johnson, the mother of Louisa, and all the children of both. Sally says Henderson is my child, but I do not believe it. Yet act of her rather than my opinion. Louisa's first child may be mine. Take care of her, and her children, who are both of *your* blood if not of mine, and of Henderson. The services of the rest will I think compensate for an indulgence to these. I cannot free these people and send them North. It would be cruelty to them. Nor would I like that any but my own blood should own as slaves my own blood or Louisa. I leave them to your charge, believing that you will best appreciate and most independently carry out my wishes in regard to them. Do not let Louisa or any of my children, or possible children, be slaves of strangers. Slavery in the family will be their happiest earthly condition.[27]

BY MIDCENTURY, THE POPULATION of the Midwest states alone equaled that of the white South. Southerners feared losing political control of their destiny within the Union. Free-soil voters had long been opposed to federal law which mandated the return of fugitive slaves; they were further outraged at the Supreme Court decision in the Dred Scott case, which stated that Congress had no right to limit the expansion of slavery into the territories. The crisis came to a head in 1860, when the Democratic Party split along sectional lines and Abe Lincoln—with a minority of the popular vote—was elected president. Seven states seceded before he even took office.

— KARL MARX: The present struggle between the North and South is, therefore, nothing but a struggle between two social systems, between the system of slavery and the system of free labor. The struggle has broken out because the two systems can no longer live peacefully side by side on the North American continent. It can only be ended by the victory of one system or the other.[28]

— REV. JAMES THORNWELL: The parties in this conflict are not merely abolitionists and slaveholders; they are atheists, socialists, communists, red republicans, jacobins on the one side, and the friends of order and regulated freedom on the other.[29]

— FREDERICK LAW OLMSTED: Will any traveler say that he has seen no signs of discontent, or insecurity, or apprehension, or precaution; that the South has appeared quieter and less excited, even on the subject of slavery, than the North; that the negroes seem happy and contented, and the citizens more tranquilly engaged in the pursuit of their business and pleasure? . . . In Richmond, and Charleston, and New Orleans, the citizens are as careless and gay as in Boston or London, and their servants a thousand times as childlike and cordial, to all appearances, in their relations with them as our servants are with us. But go to the bottom of this security and dependence, and you come to police machinery such as you never find in towns under free government: citadels, sentries, passports, grape-shotted cannon, and daily public whippings of the subjects for accidental infractions of police ceremonies. . . . Similar precautions and similar customs may be discovered in every large town in the South.[30]

— THEODORE WELD: The fact that slaveholders may be full of benevolence and kindness toward their equals and toward whites generally, even so much so as to attract the esteem and admiration of all, while they treat with the most inhuman neglect their own slaves, is well illustrated by a circumstance mentioned by the Rev. Dr. Channing, of Boston (who once lived in Virginia), in his work on slavery, p. 162, 1st edition:

> "I cannot," says the doctor, "forget my feelings on visiting a hospital belonging to the plantation of a gentleman *highly esteemed for his virtues*, and whose manners and conversation expressed much *benevolence* and *conscientiousness*. When I entered with him the hospital, the first object on which my eye fell was a young woman very ill, probably approaching death. She was stretched on the floor. Her head rested on something like a pillow, but her body and limbs were extended on the hard boards. The owner, I doubt not, had, at least, as much kindness as myself, but he was so used to see the slaves living without common comforts, that the idea of unkindness in the present instance did not enter his mind."[31]

— JUDGE NICHOLS: The deliberate convictions of my most matured consideration are, that the institution of slavery is a most serious injury to the habits, manners and morals of our *white* population; that it leads to sloth, indolence, dissipation and vice.[32]

— ALEXIS DE TOCQUEVILLE: The American of the South is fond of grandeur, luxury, and renown, of gayety, pleasure, and, above all, of idleness; nothing obliges him to exert himself in order to subsist; and as he has no necessary occupations, he gives way to indolence and does not even attempt what would be useful.[33]

— AUCTIONEER: Why, gentlemen, you kin look over this whole gang of niggers, from the oldest to the youngest, an' you won't find the mark of a whip on one of 'em. . . . These here po' devils is sold for no fault whatever, but simply and only because, owin' to the Curnel's sudden death, his estate is left embarrassed, and it is necessary to sell his niggers to pay his debts, and for distributin' some reddy monny amongst numrus 'aars. Of these facts I assure you upon the honor of a gentleman.[34]

AN ORDINANCE CONCERNING NEGROES

Be it ordained by the council of the city of Richmond, that in this ordinance, and in any future ordinance of this city, the word 'negro' shall be construed to mean mulatto as well as negro. . . .

Not more than five negroes shall at any one time stand together on a sidewalk at or near the corner of a street or public alley. And negroes shall not at any time stand on a sidewalk to the inconvenience of persons passing by. A negro meeting or overtaking, or being overtaken by a white person on a sidewalk, shall pass on the outside; and if it be necessary to enable such white person to pass, shall immediately get off the side-walk.[35]

— FREDERICK DOUGLASS: At every gate through which we were to pass, we saw a watchman—at every ferry a guard—on every bridge a sentinel—and in every wood a patrol. We were hemmed in upon every side. . . . On the one hand, there stood Slavery, a stern reality, glaring frightfully upon us—its robes already crimsoned with the blood of millions, and even now feasting itself greedily upon our own flesh. On the other hand, away back in the dim distance, under the flickering light of the north star, behind some craggy hill or snow-covered mountain, stood a doubtful freedom—half frozen—beckoning us to come and share its hospitality. . . .

Upon either side we saw grim death, assuming the most horrid shapes. Now it was starvation, causing us to eat our own flesh—now we were contending with the waves, and were drowned—now we were overtaken, and torn to pieces by the gangs of the terrible bloodhound. We were stung by scorpions, chased by wild beasts, bitten by snakes, and finally, after having nearly reached the desired spot—after swimming rivers, encountering wild beasts, bitten by snakes, sleeping in the woods, suffering hunger and nakedness—we were overtaken by our pursuers, and, in our resistance, we were shot dead upon the spot![36]

— FREDERICK LAW OLMSTED: It must be borne in mind that throughout the South slaves are accustomed to "run away." On every large or moderate plantation which I visited, I had evidence that in peace, with, south of Virginia and east of Texas, no prospect of finding shelter within hundreds of miles, or of long avoiding recapture and severe punishment, many slaves had a habit of frequently making efforts to escape temporarily from their ordinary condition of subjection. I have shown that this is so common that Southern writers gravely describe it as a disease—a monomania, to which the negro race is peculiarly subject, making the common mistake of attributing to blood that which is more rationally to be traced to condition.[37]

— FREDERICK DOUGLASS: O God, save me! God, deliver me! Let me be free! Is there any God? Why am I a slave? I will run away. I will not stand it. Get caught, or get clear, I'll try it. . . . I have only one life to lose. I had as well be killed running as die standing. Only think of it; one hundred miles straight north, and I am free! Try it? Yes! God helping me, I will. It cannot be that I shall live and die a slave.[38]

AT HEART, THE MASTER must fear the slave, "lest he ever get a gun in his hand." So white men grow a deep fear of retribution, disguised as the notion that given half a chance, black men will rape and murder their masters' wives and children—the myth of Mandingo. Black people, about 12 percent of the population in the United States, currently constitute nearly half of the total prison population—which is, consequently, among the largest in the world.

If the North fought the war to free the slaves, is this the legacy of abolition? Southside Chicago in the winter: bitterly cold with no heat in the building because the landlord turned the heat off. Kids dealing drugs on the street, packing guns to school. Kids killing kids. Kids having babies. Daddy's in prison, or dead, or gone the Lord knows where.

--- ELIJAH AVEY: He was five feet ten inches high, weighed 190 pounds, had beautiful dark brown hair and beard, both of which were a little wavy. He presented a romantic picture on the day of execution. His hair and beard had been permitted to grow and his waxen complexion was a striking contrast. He wore a black broad cloth suit, a soft hat and a pair of boots, when hanged. The clothes were a gift of his sister. He was thirty-eight years of age.[39]

--- JOHN BROWN: Had I interfered in the manner which I admit has been fairly proved . . . had I so interfered in behalf of the rich, the powerful, the intelligent, the so-called great, or in behalf of any of their friends, either father, mother, brother, sister, wife or children, or any of that class, and suffered and sacrificed what I have in this interference, it would have been all right and every man in this court would have deemed it an act worthy of reward, rather than punishment.[40]

--- CLEMENT L. VALLANDIGHAM: It is in vain to underrate either the man or the conspiracy. Capt. John Brown is as brave and resolute a man as ever headed an insurrection. He has coolness, daring, persistency, the stoic faith and patience, and a firmness of will and purpose unconquerable. He is the farthest possible removed from the ordinary ruffian, fanatic, or madman.[41]

— RICHARD TAYLOR: From selfish ambition, from thoughtless zeal, from reckless partisanship, from the low motives governing demagogues in a country of universal suffrage, men are ever sowing the wind, thinking they can control the whirlwind.[42]

— CHARLES C. COFFIN: "On to Richmond!" It was a natural cry, that slogan of the North in the early months of the war; for, in ordinary warfare, to capture an enemy's capital is equivalent to conquering a peace. It was thought that the taking of Richmond would be the end of the Rebellion. Time has disabused us of this idea. . . . The vitality of the Rebellion existed not in cities, towns, or capitals, but in that which could die only by annihilation—Human Slavery. That was and is the "original sin" of the Rebellion—the total depravity and innate heinousness, to use theological terminology, without which there could not have been treason, secession, and rebellion.[43]

— REV. PETER RANDOLPH: The scene that opened before my eyes as I entered Richmond cannot be accurately described by word or pen. The city was in smoke and ashes, that is, a goodly part of it, for the Confederacy, on taking their departure, fired the city rather than let it fall into the hands of the Union forces.

The colored people from all parts of the state were crowding in at the capital, running, leaping, and praising God that freedom had come at last. It seems to me I can hear their songs now as they ring through the air: "Slavery chain done broke at last; slavery chain done broke at last—I's goin' to praise God till I die."[44]

— RALPH WALDO EMERSON: The negro has saved himself, and the white man very patronizingly says, I have saved you.[45]

— ALEXIS DE TOCQUEVILLE: Slavery recedes, but the prejudice to which it has given birth is immovable. Whoever has inhabited the United States must have perceived that in those parts of the Union in which the Negroes are no longer slaves they have in no wise drawn nearer to the whites. On the contrary, the prejudice of race appears to be stronger in the states that have abolished slavery than in those where it still exists; and nowhere is it so intolerant as in those states where servitude has never been known. . . .

If I were called upon to predict the future, I should say that the abolition of slavery in the South will, in the common course of things, increase the repugnance of the white population for the blacks.[46]

4

Five Forks

Ellen White

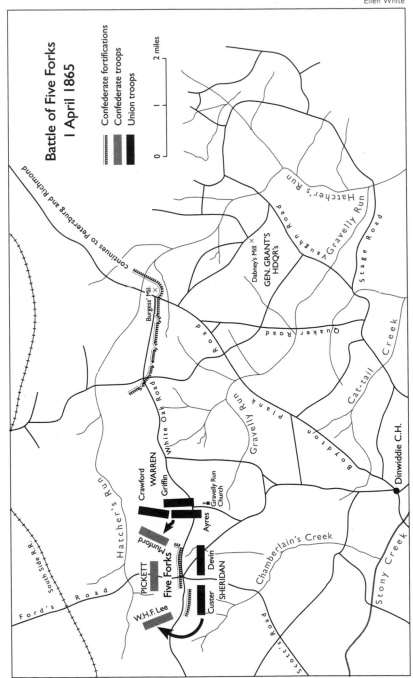

Battle of Five Forks
1 April 1865

Confederate fortifications
Confederate troops
Union troops

2 miles
1
0

continues to Petersburg and Richmond

Hatcher's Run

Gravelly Run

Stage Road

Vaughn Road

Dabney's Mill ✕
GEN. GRANT'S HDQR's

Burgess' Mill ✕

Quaker Road

Cat-tail Creek

White Oak Road

Gravelly Run

Boydton Plank Road

Dinwiddie C.H.

Crawford
WARREN
Griffin

Gravelly Run Church

Ayres

Munford

PICKETT

Five Forks

Devin

SHERIDAN

Custer

W.H.F. Lee

Ford's Road

South Side R.R.

Chamberlain's Creek

Scott's Road

Stony Creek

Brigadier General Thomas Taylor Munford commands Fitzhugh Lee's division of cavalry at Five Forks, on Pickett's left flank. As it turns out, these are the only troops standing between Pickett and disaster—and they are only able to delay disaster for a couple of hours. In so doing they allow Pickett and his cavalry commander Fitz Lee time to picnic across Hatcher's Run with their friend Tom Rosser, whose own division of cavalry is back that day guarding the wagons, and who has invited his colleagues to share his fresh fire-baked shad and apple brandy, rare delicacies in this spring of '65.

———◆———

— JOHN B. JONES: April 1st.—Clear and Pleasant. . . . We have vague and incoherent accounts from excited couriers of fighting, without result, in Dinwiddie County, near the South Side Railroad. It is rumored that a battle will probably occur in that vicinity to-day.[1]

— BUSHROD JOHNSON: On Saturday morning, the 1st of April, the enemy disappeared from the vicinity of the White Oak road, and it was discovered that they had moved toward the right. At 4 p.m. heavy firing was heard in the vicinity of Five Forks.[2]

Munford has told Fitz Lee that Yankee infantry has been spotted in the vicinity of the White Oak road, and Fitz Lee tells Munford to take his troops and go check it out. But he doesn't tell Munford where he can be found later. When Munford sees an opportunity to use artillery against the massing Fifth Corps, he requests the detachment of a couple of guns from Matt Ransom, who's commanding one of Pickett's brigades. But Ransom tells Munford that he's under Pickett's command, and without Pickett's okay he can't possibly loan his guns to the cavalry.

And none of the couriers that Munford sends out can find Pickett.

— JOSHUA L. CHAMBERLAIN: Private correspondence of Confederate officers present gives some curious details as to a shad dinner on the north side of Hatcher's Run.[3]

— THOMAS ROSSER: I had brought some excellent shad from the Nottoway River with me, and I invited General Pickett to go back and lunch with me. He promised to be with me in an hour. He and Fitz Lee came back to me. While we were at lunch couriers came from officers in command of the picket on the White Oak road and other parallel roads, reporting the advance of the enemy. Some time was spent over the lunch, during which no firing was heard, and we concluded that the enemy was not in much of a hurry to find us at Five Forks.[4]

— TOM MUNFORD: I had sent couriers and staff officers to General Pickett several times. When we had been driven two miles, I met General Pickett coming out across Hatcher's Run, going to join his command when the battle was literally over. He had not been there to participate in it.[5]

— JEFFERSON DAVIS: The purpose to reach the Roanoke River was defeated by the success of the enemy on our right flank, and it is hardly exaggerating when you speak of that *Lunch* as the ruin of the Confederacy. It certainly did, at least, hasten the catastrophe.[6]

So here they are in the woods, Rosser and Pickett and Fitz Lee, sitting by the fire as the shad bakes. (To this day in Virginia, every spring the Democrats have what they call a "shad planking," by now a hoary political tradition.)

Perhaps in this case the generals have a "shebang" in the woods: branches placed crosswise through trees to create a primitive shelter near the fire. After days of rain, it's a fine afternoon for a picnic, and they are sure the Yankees won't attack this late on a Saturday afternoon. For some reason—the thickness of the woods or the lay of the land (it *is* April Fool's Day, after all)—the picnickers don't hear the firing when it starts a couple of miles south by the White Oak road. (At the time, journalists referred to this phenomenon as an "acoustic shadow.")

— Andrew A. Humphreys: A singular circumstance connected with this battle is the fact that General Pickett was all this time, and until near the close of the action, on the north side of Hatcher's Run, where he had heard no sound of the engagement, nor had he received any information concerning it.[7]

Make no mistake about it, George Pickett is disillusioned. At forty, he's the oldest of the three (Fitz Lee is only twenty-nine; Rosser, twenty-eight)—and he's the most cynical. As a matter of fact, Fitz Lee and Rosser, and Munford as well, don't surrender at Appomattox. They want to go fight in the mountains, wage guerrilla war against the Yankees. A few days' thought, and words of counsel from Uncle Bob, convince them otherwise.

— Robert E. Lee: A partisan war may be continued, and hostilities protracted, causing individual suffering and the devastation of the country, but I see no prospect by that means of achieving a separate independence.[8]

— Spencer Glasgow Welch: We need ten or fifteen thousand more men here, and we could easily get them if the able-bodied exempts would come on here, but they seem to have become hardened to their disgrace. If the South is ever overcome, the contemptible shirkers will be responsible for it.[9]

— Jennie Hill Caldwell: What is said about evacuation in camp? It is the familiar topic here, and everybody seems determined to believe that the Yankees will get here. I have been advised to practice Yankee Doodle and the Star Spangled Banner. I think the Confederacy, without jesting, is to use a soldier phrase "gone up the spout." I still hope the Yankees may not cut us off. Everybody is more desponding than ever about the war.[10]

RICHMOND, VA., APRIL 1, 1865.

It is evidently the intention of President Davis and the Confederate Government officers to move from this city. An evacuation and surrender of the capital is not far off. The assets of the banks have been sent off by the Danville Road. . . .

Flour is fifteen hundred dollars per barrel; tea, one hundred dollars per pound; coffee, fifty dollars; bacon, eighteen dollars; beef, fifteen dollars; and eggs are this morning quoted at thirty-five dollars per dozen.[11]

Sheridan has caught Pickett and his attached cavalry out in the open. The Confederate defensive works end a few miles to the east, near Burgess' Mill. Just twenty-four hours ago, there was a morning of Federal panic as, Lee himself in command, the Confederates sally forth to turn the Union left. But by this time there are so few Southern troops—and those who do remain in the lines are so undernourished— that all Lee can accomplish is to panic one Federal division, and then the rest of the Fifth Corps arrive to force the Confederates back to their fortifications. Still, some Southerners haven't entirely lost hope.

PETERSBURG, VA., APRIL 1, 1865.

Our lines are secure against all attacks of the enemy. On the whole, all goes well with us, and ere long we hope to be able to chronicle a glorious victory for our arms and a crushing defeat to the enemy.[12]

Pickett has been told by Lee to defend Five Forks "at all hazards," though this leaves the defense of Petersburg no stronger than a picket line. Pickett's infantry has entrenched at Five Forks, but his temporary works—"just high enough to insure a death wound"—end a few miles from Lee's right, and though Pickett has requested reinforcements they will never arrive (the telegram, it seems, has gone astray).

The only Rebel troops here on Pickett's left flank are the dismounted horsemen of Munford's division, at less than half strength now, nearly four years into the war. These troopers have arrived recently, after being disbanded all winter. Since Sheridan had laid waste to the Valley of Virginia, there were no longer enough winter provisions, for men or horses, to support the cavalry.

— John B. Gordon: Heaps of ashes, of half-melted iron axles and bent tires, were the melancholy remains of burnt barns and farm-wagons and implements of husbandry. . . . At the close of this campaign of General Sheridan there was in that entire fertile valley—the former American Arcadia—scarcely a family that was not struggling for subsistence.[13]

Sheridan the Hun: it's no coincidence that in later life he would be prime architect of the military plan to slaughter the bison, thereby depriving the Plains Indians of their food supply. He died of a heart attack in 1888, at age fifty-seven, shortly after becoming commanding general of the army. Grant called Sheridan the most brilliant of his generals.

Another American "hero" in the campaign against the Indian nations also fought at Five Forks: Major General George Armstrong Custer, "Son of the Morning Star," with his long golden hair. Like Pickett, he had graduated last in his class at West Point. Custer was commander of a Federal cavalry division that "demonstrated" on Pickett's front, fixing the Confederates in place while Major General Gouverneur K. Warren's Fifth Corps infantry encircled the cavalry on the Confederate left.

On the Confederates' right flank occurred one of the largest cavalry engagements at the end of the war—two groups of horsemen riding directly at each other until they're close enough to slash each other with sabers. Here the Rebel cavalry, under the command of Major General W. H. F. "Rooney" Lee, held the Yankees at bay, allowing what remained of Pickett's broken units to retreat after sunset.

But it's on the Confederate left flank where the battle is lost.

— WILLIAM CLARK CORSON: The day I got to camp the command was ordered to report to Gen. Fitz Lee at Waynesborough. We marched down there in the night through a cold freezing rain over roads that were barely passable in the day time. We reached Waynesborough about 2 o'clock at night and went into camp cold, wet and hungry. I thought I would not live to see morning, but I did, and such a wretched scene I have never before witnessed in or out of the army. Our poor horses shivering with cold and famished with hunger were neighing piteously and biting the bark from the trees to which they were tied.

The men looking like graven images were crowded around the sickly fires that we could scarcely keep burning the rain came down in such torrents.[14]

— DAVID CARDWELL: We were up in the saddle after a hasty breakfast of grapefruit, eggs *au gratin*, hot rolls, beefsteak, German fried potatoes and coffee—I reckon not! What we had was corn pone cooked three days before and raw Nassau pork (sometimes called "mule" by the boys, who worshipped it and got so little of it). I was hungry— "hungry" is not strong enough. I was so hungry that I thanked God that I had a backbone for my stomach to lean up against.[15]

MUNFORD'S DISMOUNTED CAVALRY buy the Confederacy a bit of time, but they can't withstand the Yankee Fifth Corps even the few hours needed until sundown. (It will be dark by seven o'clock.) The Federals aren't ready to attack until nearly 4:30 in the afternoon, that Saturday, April 1st—and long before that Sheridan is fuming, pacing up and back in front of the Gravelly Run Methodist Church wondering why the hell Warren hasn't gotten his men ready to go into action yet, he can see them sitting around in the fields making coffee (as they'll do whenever they get half a chance). Finally the last troops march into place, exhausted, having been force-marched all the previous night, stopping and starting, back and forth across the muddy Virginia countryside (the bridge is out over Gravelly Run), down toward Dinwiddie Court House and then up to Five Forks.

— CHARLES C. COFFIN: A heavy rain-storm came up. Wagons went hub-deep in the mud. The swamps were overflowed. The army came to a standstill. The soldiers were without tents. Thousands had thrown away their blankets. There was gloom and discouragement through-out the camp.[16]

— ULYSSES S. GRANT: The quicksands of this section exceed anything I have ever seen. Roads have to be corduroyed in front of teams and artillery as they advance. We were fifty-six hours moving 600 teams five miles with 1,200 men to help them. Through the woods where it is perfectly dry for infantry, horses will go through so deep as to scarcely be able to extricate themselves.[17]

— GOUVERNEUR K. WARREN: The bridge is broken on the plank road, and will take I hardly know how long to make passable for infantry. . . . It requires a span of forty feet to complete the bridge, and the stream is too deep to ford.[18]

— GEORGE MEADE: A dispatch, partially transmitted, is received, indicating the bridge over Gravelly Run is destroyed, and time will be required to rebuild it. If this is the case, would not time be gained by

sending the troops by the Quaker road? Time is of the utmost importance. Sheridan cannot maintain himself at Dinwiddie without reinforcements, and yours are the only ones that can be sent. Use every
exertion to get the troops to him as soon as possible. If necessary, send
troops by both roads and give up the rear attack.[19]

— GOUVERNEUR K. WARREN: I issued my orders on General Webb's
first dispatch to fall back, which made the divisions retire in the order
of Ayres, Crawford, and Griffin, which was the order they could most
rapidly move in. I cannot change them tonight without producing confusion that will render all my operations nugatory. I will now send
General Ayres to General Sheridan, and take General Griffin and general Crawford to move against the enemy, as this last dispatch directs
I should. I cannot accomplish the apparent objects of the orders I have
received.[20]

IN FACT, EARLY IN THE MORNING of April 1st, the Confederates under Pickett—following Lee's orders to protect the crossroads—have themselves fallen back to Five Forks from near Dinwiddie Court House, where they had been threatening Sheridan. Later that same morning Grant gives Sheridan specific written permission to remove Warren as commander of the Fifth Corps, should Sheridan think it necessary. The bad feelings between Sheridan and Warren go back a long way, further even than the previous spring, when Warren was slow to bring his forces up at Spotsylvania and Cold Harbor.

> — ULYSSES S. GRANT: There was no officer more capable, nor one more prompt in acting, than Warren when the enemy forced him to it.[21]

Sheridan is a commander who accompanied Grant out of the West, and Warren was one of George McClellan's men (who himself had been removed by Lincoln for "a case of the slows"). Their conflict perhaps goes all the way back to West Point, where Warren, twenty years old at the time, graduated second in his class—but Sheridan, only a year younger but three years behind Warren in school, was in the bottom half of his. Perhaps the fastidious Warren gave Sheridan the plebe a hard time.

> — GOUVERNEUR K. WARREN: When I met General Sheridan, at about 11 A.M., his manner was cordial and friendly. I had never served with him before.[22]

> — ULYSSES S. GRANT: He was very impatient to make the assault and have it all over before night. . . . He sent staff officer after staff officer in search of Warren, directing that general to report to him, but they were unable to find him.[23]

→ PHIL SHERIDAN: I was exceedingly anxious to attack at once, for the sun was getting low, and we had to fight or go back. It was no place to intrench, and it would have been shameful to have gone back with no results to compensate for the loss of the brave men who had fallen during the day. In this connection, I will say that General Warren did not exert himself to get up his corps as rapidly as he might have done, and his manner gave me the impression that he wished the sun to go down before dispositions for the attack could be completed.[24]

→ GOUVERNEUR K. WARREN: While the troops were forming I told General Sheridan it would occupy till 4 P.M., at which time they *were* formed, and at which time the sun was *two and a half hours high.* Certainly I could not have expected the sun to go down before the "dispositions for the attack could be completed," nor have given him reason to think I wished it. I had at the time confidence in the success of our proposed attack, and the kindest feelings toward General Sheridan, under whom I was glad to serve. I am utterly at a loss to account for the misapprehension he labored under in imputing such baseness to me, and I trust my conduct throughout the war has shown to those by whom I am best known that I am incapable of it.[25]

AT FOUR IN THE AFTERNOON, General Warren's troops are finally up by the Gravelly Run Church, and Sheridan points out with a sword in the dust—it's been sunny all day long and some of the mud has dried out—Sheridan sketches in the dust his and Grant's great plan to collapse Lee's right and force the Army of Northern Virginia out into the open. In this way they will force Lee to abandon the long line of earthworks—seemingly impregnable—stretching thirty-five miles from Richmond all the way south to Burgess' Mill and points west. By capturing Five Forks, Sheridan will be able to control the South Side Railroad, Lee's last escape line west, lying just a couple of miles up the Ford road.

— JOSHUA L. CHAMBERLAIN: The plan in general was for the cavalry to occupy the enemy's attention by a brisk demonstration along the right front of their works, while the Fifth Corps should fall upon their left and rear, by a sort of surprise if possible, and scoop them out of their works along the White Oak road, and capture or disorganize them.[26]

— PHIL SHERIDAN: This battle must be fought and won before the sun goes down. All the conditions may be changed in the morning. We have but a few hours of daylight left us.[27]

After the battle, Sheridan will report to Grant that five thousand Rebel troops are captured at Five Forks—more than 10 percent of what remains of Lee's army. Knowing that the Confederate lines around Petersburg will no longer hold, Grant immediately orders a general assault. Richmond is doomed.

— PHIL SHERIDAN: The enemy made a last stand at the Five Forks behind a strong line of earthworks along the White Oak road. After forcing them to this position, I directed General Merritt to push his dismounted cavalry well up to the enemy's works and drive in their skirmishers and make the enemy believe that our main attack would be made on their right flank. In the meantime I had ordered up the

Fifth Corps to within a mile of the Five Forks on the Dinwiddie Court House road, for the purpose of attacking the enemy's left flank and rear. Between 4 and 5 o'clock, in accordance with these dispositions, the Fifth Corps moved out across the White Oak road, swinging round to the left as they advanced, and struck the enemy in flank and rear. Simultaneously with this attack the cavalry assaulted the enemy's works in front in compliance with my orders to General Merritt, and the result of this combined movement was the complete rout of the enemy with the loss of 5 pieces of artillery and caissons, a number of their wagons and ambulances, and I think at least 5,000 prisoners and several battle-flags.[28]

— ROBERT E. LEE: A large force of infantry, believed to be the Fifth Corps, with other troops, turned General Pickett's left and drove him back on the White Oak road, separating him from General Fitz Lee, who was compelled to fall back across Hatcher's Run. General Pickett's present position is not known.[29]

AT THE END OF THE DAY, Sheridan does in fact relieve Warren of command, because, according to Sheridan, he "wasn't in the thick of the fight." Warren has spent all afternoon chasing General Crawford, who, instead of attacking Pickett's infantry behind their meager entrenchments at Five Forks, gets sidetracked in the woods fighting Tom Munford's dismounted cavalry. The Fifth Corps loses more than six hundred men in the battle, half of those from Crawford's Third Division.

— PHIL SHERIDAN: During this attack I again became dissatisfied with General Warren. During the engagement, portions of his line gave way when not exposed to a heavy fire, and simply from want of confidence on the part of the troops, which General Warren did not exert himself to inspire. I therefore relieved him from the command of the Fifth Corps, authority for this action having been sent to me before the battle, unsolicited.[30]

For years after the war, the old soldiers of the Fifth Corps will gather at Warren's house in Newport to "fight the war" again. Dr. Louis Manarin, the Virginia state archivist—who wrote his master's thesis on Warren and the battle of Five Forks (and his doctoral dissertation on General Lee)—tells me this one afternoon, in his office in the Virginia State Library dominated by Everett B. D. Julio's wall-size painting, *The Last Meeting of Lee and Jackson.*

When she was an old woman, Warren's daughter told Manarin that she remembered hearing the men talk around the kitchen table about how Crawford was always getting her father into trouble. Of course, the numbers speak for themselves: Crawford's division lost more than either of the other Fifth Corps divisions, so it's probably not fair to say that they weren't in the thick of the fight. But there was already a lot of bad blood between Warren and Sheridan, and Sheridan had the absurd expectation—since that's what Grant had wired him—that Warren would have his troops on the field by noon.

— JOSHUA L. CHAMBERLAIN: All is lost; and all is won. Slowly Warren returns over the somber field. At its forsaken edge a staff officer hands him a crude field order. Partly by the lurid flashes of the last guns, partly by light of the dying day, he reads:

> Major-General Warren, commanding the Fifth Army Corps, is relieved from duty and will at once report for orders to Lieutenant-General Grant, commanding Armies of the United States.
>
> *By command of Major-General Sheridan*

With almost the agony of death on his face, Warren approaches Sheridan and asks him if he cannot reconsider the order.

— PHIL SHERIDAN: Reconsider. Hell! I don't reconsider my decisions. Obey the order![31]

For fourteen years after the war ends, Warren—a career army engineer—keeps attempting to get his case heard before a court of inquiry. But Grant is so hostile to Warren, and as president is so influential, that Warren doesn't get his hearing until nearly three years after Grant leaves office. Not until 1882 is the business finished. The court does in the end vindicate Warren, but there's a lengthy "delay" before the court's report is published, and by then it's too late for him: Warren is already in his grave. Gouverneur Warren was buried, as he stipulated, in civilian dress.

Today there's a monument at Gettysburg, on Little Round Top, of General Warren in uniform. The second day at Gettysburg, the day before Pickett's charge, Warren pulled the Federal bacon out of the fire: seeing that Little Round Top was undefended, he ordered troops there (including Joshua Chamberlain's Maine regiment), just in time to stop General John Bell Hood's Texans from getting cannon to the Top, from which point they could have blasted away at the entire Union line.

— GOUVERNEUR K. WARREN: At my suggestion, General Meade sent me
to the left to examine the condition of affairs, and I continued on till I
reached Little Round Top. There were no troops on it, and it was used
as a signal station. I saw that this was the key of the whole position, and
that our troops in the woods in front of it could not see the ground in
front of them, so that the enemy would come upon them before they
would be aware of it.

The long line of woods on the west side of the Emmitsburg road
(which road was along a ridge) furnished an excellent place for the
enemy to form out of sight, so I requested the captain of a rifle battery just in front of Little Round Top to fire a shot into these woods.
He did so, and as the shot went whistling through the air the sound
of it reached the enemy's troops and caused every one to look in the
direction of it. This motion revealed to me the glistening of gun-bar-
rels and bayonets of the enemy's line of battle, already formed and far
outflanking the position of any of our troops; so that the line of his
advance from his right to Little Round Top was unopposed. I have
been particular in telling this, as the discovery was intensely thrilling
to my feelings, and almost appalling.

I immediately sent a hastily written dispatch to General Meade to
send a division at least to me, and General Meade directed the Fifth
Army Corps to take position there. The battle was already beginning
to rage at the Peach Orchard, and before a single man reached Round
Top the whole line of the enemy moved on us in splendid array, shouting in the most confident tones. . . .

About this time First Lieutenant Charles E. Hazlett of the Fifth
Artillery, with his battery of rifled cannon, arrived. He comprehended
the situation instantly and planted a gun on the summit of the hill. He
spoke to the effect that though he could do little execution on the
enemy with his guns, he could aid in giving confidence to the infantry,
and that his battery was of no consequence whatever compared
with holding the position. He stayed there till he was killed.[32]

BACK TO APRIL FOOL'S DAY, 1865, nearly two long years after Gettysburg. SHAD BAKE DESTROYS CONFEDERACY. Grant maneuvers Lee out of Richmond, a strategic exercise that would have been admired by Clausewitz. The long thin gray line breaks at last. The starving Army of Northern Virginia is overwhelmed by the blue tide off the Potomac.

— HORACE PORTER: About one o'clock it was reported by the cavalry that the enemy was retiring to his entrenched position at Five Forks, which was just north of the White Oak road and parallel to it, his earthworks running from a point about three quarters of a mile east of Five Forks to a point a mile west, with an angle or "crochet," about one hundred yards long, thrown back at right angles to the left of his line to protect that flank. Orders were at once given to Warren's corps to move up the Gravelly Run Church road to the open ground near the church, and form in order of battle, with Ayres on the left, Crawford on his right, and Griffin in rear as a reserve. The corps was to wheel to the left and make its attack upon the angle, and then, moving westward, sweep down in rear of the enemy's entrenched line.[33]

By the time the Feds attack, the sun is barely over the tree line at the edge of the field. The Third Division crosses the White Oak road in line of battle at the junction of the Gravelly Run Church road. The sight of a Civil War division strung out across more than a mile of ground is something only hinted at nowadays in reenactments.

Though there were photographers in the war, newspapers and magazines still used woodcuts and sketches drawn from life as illustrations—and in any case the photographic plates available at the time were too slow for anything but carefully staged, static scenes. It wasn't until years later that most of the American public saw photos of the war, and in the meantime many irreplaceable photographic plates ended up as part of a greenhouse roof.

There's a drawing in the Library of Congress by the artist Alfred Waud, a sketch of Federal infantry attacking at Five Forks. Regiments and brigades, battle flags flying, they advance in an orderly line of two ranks, one just behind the other. The sun is still above the trees as the Federal troops cross the White Oak road and swing to the left. There's about a hundred yards of open field between the road and the thick woods, and the Yankees haven't gone far before Munford's dismounted troopers open fire from the tree line.

— JOHN C. GOOLSBY: Look with me, my comrades, as I attempt to picture to you this beautiful field, the foliage of which was now bursting out in all its glory . . . now so peaceful, yet soon to be the seat of carnage.[34]

Though the Fifth Corps has been instructed to keep the sun in its eyes, heading west toward the fortifications at Five Forks proper, the fire from Munford's cavalry is coming from the northwest. The Yankee Third Division, Crawford's division, starts turning to the right to engage the Confederates. The First Brigade, which contains the Sixth and Seventh Wisconsin Volunteer Regiments, crosses the corn-stubble field in the bright fading April afternoon. By the time they get across the split rail fence and into the woods, they are drawing a heavy fire from the dismounted Virginia cavalry.

— TOM MUNFORD: The air was now filled with the "sweet mysterious singing" and whining of rifle bullets. They seemed to come whistling and gurgling from every direction, or buzzing like angry bees ere they struck among the pines. Suddenly two full divisions of Warren's Corps, Crawford's and Ayres', debouched upon the White Oak Road. They were in magnificent array, exposing a full front probably one thousand yards long—as tempting a target as ever stood before a soldier's guns. . . .

Perceiving that we were in the woods in front of him, Crawford moved straight at us while Ayres wheeled to his left and went at Ransom. The battle was on in deadly earnest now. I had about 1200 carbines, though all of them did not at any time get into line, and they were popping merrily. And there, right in front of us, 12,000 infantry and 2,000 cavalry were within less than two hundred yards! It was indeed a glorious target.[35]

MEANWHILE, BACK IN THE WOODS by Hatcher's Run, it's a fine spring evening, the sun just setting now through the thick pines. The air is balmy, temperature still in the seventies. The blue Virginia sky is luminous with spring. The forsythia are out, and the daffodils are spots of yellow throughout the woods, as though someone has walked by and planted them. There's a cardinal singing; there are red and white dogwood blossoms in the middle distance. The air is sweet and mild, smelling of damp earth: the smell of new green shoots pushing through last year's dead leaves. It has been a fine afternoon for a picnic.

Now that the sun's beginning to set, the air is turning a little cooler—but any chill is offset by the fire. There's a half dozen men around the fire: smelly, dirty, unshaven men in motley uniforms ragged now after nearly four years of fighting. Though the troops approaching through the woods have blue uniforms new this spring, there are no new uniforms for the Rebels—just handfuls of parched corn to be shared with the horses.

The planks on which the shad baked are cooking off in the fire, grease crackling away like the sound of distant gunfire. Pickett has long hair, now curling unwashed over the collar of his gray uniform. *Pass the schnapps. That shad tastes right fine. And I sure am tired of this goddamn war. . . .*

The first sign these men have that something is wrong occurs when they send out a pair of couriers to find out what's happening down by Five Forks. As the first courier crosses Hatcher's Run by the ford, the generals see bluecoats coming out of the woods. The courier is captured. Holy shit! Who the hell are those folks? Why, it's those guys in the black hats from the old Iron Brigade. Pickett jumps on his horse. Hold them back just a minute, he says to Captain Breckinridge of the Second Virginia Cavalry. Breckinridge rides at the Yankee infantry and gets shot out of the saddle, but Pickett—leaning over his horse's neck the way he learned from the Indians out West, before the war—makes it through the Federal fire. He's off to try to rescue the situation at Five Forks.

⟶ WALTER HARRISON: Situated in a flat, thickly-wooded country, Five Forks, as its name indicates, is simply a crossing, at nearly right angles, of two country roads, and the deflection of a third road bisecting one of those angles. A line of battle, upon the White Oak road, short as four small brigades' front must be, can readily be turned on either flank by a larger attacking force.[36]

— Samuel Crawford: We encountered the enemy's skirmishers shortly after moving, driving them steadily back. Our way led through bogs, tangled woods, and thickets of pine, interspersed with open spaces here and there.[37]

— Fitzhugh Lee: Everything continued quiet until about 3 P.M., when reports reached me of a large body of infantry marching around and menacing our left flank. I ordered Munford to go in person, ascertain the exact condition of affairs, hold his command in readiness, and if necessary order it up at once. He soon sent for it, and it reached its position just in time to receive the attack. A division of two small brigades of cavalry was not able long to withstand the attack of a Federal corps of infantry, and that force soon crushed in Pickett's left flank, swept it away.[38]

— Albert Stickney (counsel for Gouverneur K. Warren): When you met General Pickett he was coming from Hatcher's Run. Do you recollect particularly how you first saw him, or where you first saw him?[39]

— Tom Munford: Yes; I was very anxious to see General Pickett. I had sent three or four staff officers to him, advising him of the condition of things, but had no reply. He had not come up. . . . I sent my inspector-general, Capt. Henry C. Lee, who was General Robert E. Lee's nephew, to see Pickett himself, and tell him the condition of things. I sent several staff officers, but nobody came to my relief. I felt alarmed about the condition of things, because there did not seem to be any general officer there who was controlling the infantry movements. . . . The Fifth Corps was on our flank, moving, and there was no support for Fitz Lee's division of cavalry. . . .

The woods were thick; it was interspersed with little ravines full of springs, and it was very boggy. The land was natural loam. There were but few roads at Hatcher's Run. It is generally a boggy country, and the most indifferent land for cavalry to move in, and in those low points you could not move many infantry. Our horse artillery, which generally went everywhere with us, we did not dare carry in there, simply because they would have been stuck there.

— ALBERT STICKNEY: How possible was it to keep up any regular formation, in making an advance through those woods, under fire?

— TOM MUNFORD: The Fifth Corps seemed to move together, and we were scattered along, taking advantage of every obstacle that was in our favor, so as to keep up the firing; and they seemed to move very steadily. We always had a pretty good mark to fire at.

— ALBERT STICKNEY: If you had any conversation with General Pickett, when you met him at the Ford road, you may repeat it, unless you prefer not.

— TOM MUNFORD: If you don't want me to say it, I prefer not.

— ALBERT STICKNEY: Well, we do not ask for it then.

ONE AFTERNOON I PUT the dog in my car and take the interstate twenty miles south from Richmond. It's peculiar weather for Virginia, the end of March and it has just started snowing heavily. The snow is melting as it hits the pavement, but to the side of the highway I see snow sticking on the flat woods and fields of Southside Virginia. The crowded multilane highway shoots straight down to Petersburg.

After about half an hour, I'm at the Petersburg exit. I find myself driving through a neighborhood of storefront churches and bars. It reminds me of the South End of Boston, where I worked on voter registration the sooty hot summer of 1965, just one hundred years after Lee's surrender at Appomattox (it took a hundred years for Congress to pass the Voting Rights Act). Next to a line of buildings in varying stages of decay—paint peeling, boarded-up windows—I stop to read a historical marker that indicates where Lee lived during the siege, right here where this stately but now decayed brick Victorian sits (having long since replaced the actual house Lee lived in), across the street from a Pentecostal church and an all-night grocery store.

In the summer of 1965, the summer Watts burned, Lyndon Johnson began a massive call-up of troops to send to Vietnam. (Some people saw a connection between the two events: get the brothers off the streets and over there to die protecting American corporate interests in Southeast Asia.) I remember Johnson slowly swaying back and forth on the TV screen, like a snake in front of a bird.

That was *my* generation's war, the war that, to be honest, I did my damnedest to avoid. I remember watching the war on TV, my mother and father and I sitting around the kitchen table, eating dinner, watching the *CBS Evening News with Walter Cronkite.* I remember sitting at the dinner table watching men being carried on stretchers, screaming because they'd just had a foot or leg blown off by a mine, Dan Rather on the scene doing a running commentary. Just as the Civil War was the first war to be photographed, so was Vietnam the first war to be shown on television—the first war with instant replay.

My own generation's war, like most wars, was fought in the main by those too powerless to do anything other than join the army. I remember one issue of *Life* magazine, the summer of 1969 (after Vietnam had become Richard Nixon's war), which published all the pictures of one week's

American dead. Most of the faces were white kids from small towns and black kids from big cities: *A rich man's war and a poor man's fight.*

I had a medical condition—a bad back—that kept me out of the army, so I myself have never been in a war, never "seen the elephant," as Civil War vets used to say about combat. (To get into the circus tent, as a kid, you could either pay or shovel manure—in the latter case, you would indeed have a good vantage point from which to "see the elephant," though at considerable risk to life and limb. More than a few children were crushed by the large beasts.)

But to be truthful, I come from a long line of deserters and draft evaders. My father's father left Russia rather than go east as cannon fodder in the Russo-Japanese War. He was a tailor whose job in the Russian army was making officers' uniforms, and the night before he was to be shipped east his superior officer told him to go missing if he knew what was good for him. Several years later, Harry had saved up enough money in Boston to bring the rest of his family over from Russia.

My father, Harry's son, one of the generation that fought the "Good War," managed to avoid military service since as a physician he had a stateside job that was deemed essential. Though that didn't stop him from being touched by the war: while training other doctors how to respond to poison gas, outdoors in strong winds and freezing temperatures—a fluke accident—he was hit in the eye by a droplet of unevaporated mustard gas. Fortunately the playground in western Massachusetts where this exercise took place had a water fountain that for some reason had been left running during the winter, and my father saved his eye by immediately sticking his face in the icy water.

I can imagine it vividly: the bleak white field, the gray tree line with the northwest wind coming out of the frozen oaks, brown leaves rustling in the wintry air. . . .

On one side of my family—so the story has it—my thrice-great-grandfather sewed Napoleon a suit of clothes on his way through East Prussia. At that same time, not so many miles away, another ancestor, a teacher, was killed "in a dispute" with two of Napoleon's foot soldiers. As my father used to say, this tale in itself contains the history of the world.

FROM PETERSBURG I CONTINUE driving to Five Forks. I pass over the Appomattox River—a flash of twisting flat water seen out of the corner of my eye—and soon I'm on a country road driving west. By now the snow has nearly stopped falling, though it's still a gray, overcast day. The woods are a mixture of twisted bare trees and dark pines, the fields covered with snow.

I pass a spot where a creek has been dammed to form a small lake upstream. There's a "for sale" sign on the property, and I turn into the driveway. I get out of the car and stretch. The snow has stopped and there's a mist forming above the lake. In the silence of the morning I can hear the wet-pavement sounds of cars and trucks slapping by on the interstate a few miles away, the sound particularly clear under the low overcast.

This is Burgess' Mill, the southernmost extension of Lee's fortifications from Petersburg, where the lines turned west, more or less following Hatcher's Run and guarding the South Side Railroad.

Looking at the hand-painted sign, "30 Acres with Cabins," I imagine myself proprietor of the Burgess Mill Theme Park And Overnight Cabins. Just a short stop off the freeway on the way to Florida or the Smokies, folks could take a break here when the kids got too antsy. "Just a minute or two more, Johnny, Susie, soon we'll be south of Petersburg and then we can stop for burgers and shakes at the Civil War Theme Park." Every afternoon there could be a reenactment of the Battle of Hatcher's Run—more of a skirmish, really, fought at this very spot (*February 1865 . . . the last winter of the Confederacy*). Later the actor-soldiers would rise from the dead, still in costume, and visit with the tourists. The rest of the day they could demonstrate Civil War skills: muzzle loading, dyeing homespun cloth butternut-gray, and so forth. There could be display cases filled with weapons and primitive surgical tools: *The first war fought with modern weapons and the last with medieval medicine.*

Standing near my car in the still morning, hearing the hum of the nearby freeway, I find myself thinking: It's also the last major war to be fought before the Age of the Automobile—that is, one of the last nonmechanized wars, in which an army can, generally speaking, move no faster than its feet, since the railroad doesn't usually run to the battlefield. It's also the last "gentleman's war," when owning a horse—particularly in the Confederate cavalry, where both officers and men supplied their own mounts—would allow a fellow to remain a cut above the foot sloggers.

— WILLIAM T. SHERMAN: The young bloods of the South, sons of planters, lawyers about town, good billiard players, and sportsmen— men who never did work nor never will. War suits them, and the rascals are brave: fine riders, bold to rashness, and dangerous subjects in every sense. . . . They hate Yankees *per se*, and don't bother their brains about the past, present, or future. As long as they have good horses, plenty of forage, and an open country, they are happy. . . . This class of men must all be killed or employed by us before we can hope for peace.[40]

— JOSEPH ROBERTS: Suppose cavalry to be advancing to attack infantry, and first observed at the distance of a mile, passing over the first half mile at a trot, the next quarter of a mile at the maneuvering gallop, terminating with the charge; occupying altogether about six minutes: during the last 1500 yards of their advance how many rounds per piece might a battery fire in that time?

Eleven rounds with effect, thus:
From 1500 to 650 yards
3 min, 32 sec—spherical case 7
From 650 to 350
0 min, 48 sec—solid shot 2
From 350 to close quarters
0 min, 34 sec—canister . . . . 2 [41]

My mother's maternal grandfather was also an immigrant, from a small town near Cracow, the youngest and, no doubt about it, the wildest of three sons. Max left home when he was fourteen, in 1862, to come to Meadville, Pennsylvania, where his brother was already set up as a pharmacist. Two years later he went abroad once more, and after visiting his parents back home one last time (they both died soon after), he spent the rest of the war in London, learning the typesetter's trade.

After the Civil War, Max returned to the States and worked for a while for Horace Greeley's *New York Tribune*, before moving to Cleveland and then St. Louis, where he worked in advertising, the nineteenth century's new profession. From St. Louis, Max took his growing family (six girls and two boys) to the frontier town of Kansas City, Missouri, where he went into the liquor business. At that time Kansas was a dry state, but it was possible to deliver liquor by mail order from across the border in Missouri, which is what Max did until his death in the flu epidemic shortly before Prohibition. (He was one of millions: more people worldwide died of influenza than were killed in the Great War.)

I have always suspected that one reason Max left Pennsylvania in 1864, just two years after he had arrived, was that he had lied about his age in order to enter the country, and was about to be drafted that summer when the Federal armies needed an influx of fresh flesh for U. S. Grant's summertime campaign.

⟶ Judge Thomas Mellon: It is only greenhorns who enlist. You can learn nothing in the army. . . . Here there is no credit attached to going. All now stay if they can and go if they must. Those who are able to pay for substitutes, do so, and no discredit attaches. In time you will come to understand and believe that a man may be a patriot without risking his own life or sacrificing his health. There are plenty of other lives less valuable or others ready to serve for the love of serving.[42]

At that time, western Pennsylvania was in the midst of an economic boom. Just as ten or fifteen years earlier, the discovery of gold brought thousands of people to California, so now the nation's increasing need for oil brought thousands to the so-called Petroleum Region of Pennsylvania. All the machines in all the factories that supplied the vast Federal armies with weapons and wagons and so forth—all those machines had a vast hunger for oil to lubricate innumerable moving parts.

— JOHN S. SCHOOLEY: Oil Creek, which has become celebrated as the site of the richest oil-producing region on earth at the present day, is a tortuous mountain stream, taking its rise in the northern part of the State of Pennsylvania. . . .

The valley through which Oil Creek takes its course is narrow, and flanked on each side by high and rugged hills, on the top of which are broad fields of excellent farming land. The scenery on Oil Creek at one time, no doubt, was quite picturesque; but now the bottom lands are dotted with tall derricks, wooden engine-houses, and iron smoke-stacks, out of which columns of black smoke roll upward to the clouds. The pines and hemlock are cleared from the mountain sides, and all is busy life.[43]

Max's daughter married a man whose mother came from Kentucky. This is the Southern branch of my family, which in all of Kentucky, near as I can tell, stems from one landless heir who left Virginia in the beginning of the nineteenth century. My great-grandmother was born in Lexington on the very day, according to family legend, that the Confederate cavalry under John Morgan staged a brief and daring raid. After the war, her father—a businessman whose activities during the conflict have gone unrecorded—moved his household to Chicago, complete with "servant and six pickaninnies," as one old letter says. Thus, as I discovered, I myself—like many other Americans, both black and white—am descended from a slave owner.

— CHARLOTTE FORTEN: Fifteen of the people on this place escaped from the mainland, last spring. Among them was a man named Michael.

After they had gone some distance—their masters in pursuit—Michael's master overtook him in the swamp. A fierce grapple ensued—the master on horseback, the man on foot; the former drew a pistol and shot the slave through the arm, shattering it dreadfully. Still the brave man fought desperately and at last succeeded in unhorsing the master, and beat him until he was senseless. He then with the rest of the company escaped. With them was a woman named Rina. . . . She was overtaken by her master's cousin, and nearly run over by his horse. But he, having a liking for her, wheeled his horse around, when he saw who it was, without saying a word, and allowed her to escape. A story which I record because it is a rare thing to hear anything good of a rebel.[44]

— JEFFERSON DAVIS (*from a letter he received*):
"Excellency Davis:

"It is with feelings of undeveloped pleasure that an affectionate conscript intrusts this sheet of confiscated paper to the tender mercies of a Confederate States mail-carrier, addressed as it shall be to yourself, O Jeff, Red Jacket of the Gulf and Chief of the Six Nations, more or less. . . . It is with intense and multifariously proud satisfaction that he gazes for the last time upon our holy flag—that symbol and sign of an adored trinity, cotton, niggers, and chivalry. . . .

"And now, bastard President of a political abortion, farewell. . . . Except it be in the army of the Union, you will not again see this conscript."[45]

— THOMAS WENTWORTH HIGGINSON: Many things glide by without time to narrate them. On Saturday we had a mail with the President's Second Message of Emancipation, and the next day it was read to the men. The words themselves did not stir them very much, because they have been often told that they were free, especially on New-Year's Day, and, being unversed in politics, they do not understand, as well as we do, the importance of each additional guaranty. But the chaplain spoke to them afterwards very effectively, as usual; and then I proposed to them to hold up their hands and pledge themselves to be faithful to those still in bondage. They entered heartily into this, and the scene was quite impressive, beneath the great oak-branches.

I heard afterwards that only one man refused to raise his hand, saying bluntly that his wife was out of slavery with him, and he did not care to fight. The other soldiers of his company were very indignant, and shoved him about among them while marching back to their quarters, calling him "Coward." I was glad of their exhibition of feeling, though it is very possible that the one who had thus the moral courage to stand alone among his comrades might be more reliable, in a pinch, than some who yielded a more ready assent.[46]

BY THE TIME I GET TO Five Forks, the sky is darker than ever and it has started snowing again. The corn stubble is brown, poking up through the snow, and there are dark green pines scattered throughout the bare woods. I'm amazed how much the countryside reminds me of northern Wisconsin.

Five Forks is now—as it was a hundred years ago—a country cross-roads. I stop the car and get out to walk around, though I can't step off the asphalt without slush getting into my shoes (I've left my boots back home with the winter). It's beginning to snow more heavily; I can barely see the trees at the edge of the field across the road.

There are two small buildings here at the intersection—the Five Forks Hunt Club, a two-story frame structure, and across the road from it a cabin that appears abandoned. There's also a granite monument at one corner, four or five feet high, with chiseled words that express the grateful appreciation felt by the people of Dinwiddie County for the boys who fought and died at Five Forks, outnumbered five to one, attempting to hold off from the South Side Railroad a vastly superior Union Force.

FIFTH ARMY CORPS, APRIL 1, 1865.

5:30 o'clock, P.M. A desperate battle is now raging, with our forces advancing steadily. The enemy are fighting bravely, but are yielding slowly, while our troops are taking every advantage possible.[47]

— GEORGE PICKETT: Charge after charge of the enemy was repulsed; but they still kept pouring up division after division, and pressing round our left.[48]

My dog walks around Five Forks with me, and the hounds in their kennel at the Five Forks Hunt Club break the silence of the snowy after-noon by barking at her: Yankee Dog, Yankee Dog, what you doin' here in the South, bringing your cold and snowy weather, desecrating the holy spot where our ten thousand boys and masters—the great Virginian Pickett in command—held off the fifty-thousand Yankee horde under Little Phil the Barbarian. What you doin' here, Yankee Dog? Git back home where you belong. Now git!

— TOM MUNFORD: But what could we do? A handful to a houseful! We could do nothing but shoot and run. At their first fire the smoke enveloped them completely, and as soon as it drifted so that we could see them advancing again, we poured into them our salute of death— then turned and scooted through the woods like a flock of wild turkeys. . . .

On all sides the battle raged now. My men though scattered like wild turkeys came together again like wild turkeys at the bugle's call; the sharp cracking of their carbines was answered as they fell into skirmish line, now firing, now retreating as it became necessary to elude their pursuers. Many were crack shots, indeed, and unless their bullets struck the trees it was Crawford's disordered masses which caught them. Over to the right we could hear the hot volleys of Ransom and Wallace, and now MacGregor's Horse Artillery, with Ransom, began to boom; shells went shrieking and screeching through the air or dropped with a long, mellifluous *wh-o-o-o-m!* into the tops of the mourning pines.

Soon came the great bursting fusillade of Pickett's whole line; then the roar of gallant Pegram's thunderous guns and the crashing of Torbert's ten thousand carbines gave volume to the tumultuous voice of battle. The earth trembled under the shocks of the thundering guns; rolling volutes of sulfurous smoke wreathed the trees in ghostly, trailing garments. The low sun showed faintly through the smoke-clouds like a pale moon and the woods were stifled in their sulfurous draperies. No enemy was in sight, because of the smoke, but still the hellish din of war arose on every hand, the deadly balls spat against the boughs or whined like pettish voices above our heads. Occasionally a man crumpled down in his place and a little rivulet of blood trickled away on the ground. It was bloody war.[49]

— GEORGE PICKETT: Our loss in killed and wounded was heavy, and yet . . . with all the odds against us, we might possibly have held out till night, which was fast approaching, but that our ammunition was exhausted. We yielded to an overwhelming force, Sheridan's cavalry alone numbering more than double my whole command, with Warren's infantry corps to back them.[50]

— CORDELIA STROTHER WELCH: You ask if I have heard a battle. Only once since I came here has there been one, and 'tho Gen. Lee said of it: "Our loss was small; that of the enemy not great," nevertheless several were killed on our side, one of them being Pegram of Virginia. His young bride who was in Petersburg, knowing that he was in the neighborhood of the firing, went out, when it ceased, to meet him, as she supposed, flushed with success. Instead she met his dead body being borne back.[51]

— MARY CHESNUT: Things are beginning to be unbearable. Sit down— be satisfied. Your husband is safe—so far. Be thankful it is no worse with you.

But there is the gnawing pain all the same. What is the good of being here at all? Our world has gone to destruction.[52]

— GEORGE PICKETT: Oh, this is all a weary, long mistake.[53]

— JOSHUA L. CHAMBERLAIN (*from a letter he received*): "I rested my gun on the rock and took steady aim. I started to pull the trigger, but some queer notion stopped me. Then I got ashamed of my weakness and went through the same motions again. I had you, perfectly certain. But that same queer something shut right down on me. I couldn't pull the trigger, and gave it up—that is, your life. I am glad of it now, and hope you are."[54]

5

Calhoun's Monument

Richmond, Va. Ruins of the Gallego Flour Mill; a later view. Photograph by Alexander Gardner, April 1965. Library of Congress, Prints and Photographs Division, LC-B8171-7031.

The sun has set in Virginia. This fine spring day is drawing to a close. The limpid light is fading, the air soft and faintly sweet-smelling. But the afternoon that was so perfect for a picnic, the first really nice day of the year, has been disturbed by the mayhem of battle, the rolling thunder of artillery and rifle fire. Men have been murdering each other up and down these woods and fields. And now, with darkness, it's coming to an end. Vastly superior Federal forces have defeated Pickett's Confederates. It's over.

— Charles C. Coffin: "We have only to resolve that we will never surrender, and it will be impossible that we shall ever be taken," said the *Sentinel*, in its issue of Saturday morning, April 1st, the last paper ever issued from that office. The editor was not aware of the fact that on Friday evening, while he was penning this paragraph, Sheridan was bursting open the door at the Five Forks and had the Rebellion by the throat.[1]

RICHMOND, VA., APRIL 1, 1865.

The weather is cool and pleasant. Excited couriers have arrived from off the line of the South Side Railroad and report the Yankees as fighting their way through our lines, and their numbers as so great that we cannot much longer hold Petersburg.

The number of Virginians reported absent from their regiments without leave, will, this morning, exceed fifty thousand. What can this mean? A few more days will certainly decide as to whether we will succeed in longer holding together the Confederacy.[2]

— George Alfred Townsend: Now Richmond rocked in her high towers to watch the impending issue, but soon the day began to look gray, and a pale moon came tremulously out to watch the meeting squadrons. Imagine along a line of a full mile, thirty thousand men struggling for life and prestige; the woods gathering about them—but yesterday the home of hermit hawks and chipmunks—now ablaze with bursting shells, and showing in the dusk the curl of flames in the tangled grass, and, rising up the boles of the pine trees, the scaling, scorching tongues. Seven hours this terrible spectacle had been enacted, but the finale of it had almost come.[3]

⏤ GOUVERNEUR K. WARREN: General Crawford's troops soon encountered a stiff line of the enemy, formed to meet him. . . . The contest, however, was short, for the enemy, now pressed front, flank and rear, mostly threw down their arms.[4]

⏤ GEORGE PICKETT: I rode straight up to where they were and joined in singing, "Rally once again," as I waved the blood-stained flag. . . . overpowered, defeated, cut to pieces, starving, captured, as we were, those that were left of us formed front and north and south, and met with sullen desperation their double onset.[5]

⏤ CHARLES C. COFFIN: In an hour the C.S.A.—the Confederate Slave Argosy—the Ship of State launched but four years ago, which went proudly sailing, with the death's-head and cross-bones at her truck, on a cruise against Civilization and Christianity . . . was thrown a helpless wreck upon the shores of Time![6]

⏤ GEORGE PICKETT: Charge after charge was made and repulsed, and division after division of the enemy advanced upon us. Our left was turned; we were completely entrapped.[7]

⏤ GOUVERNEUR K. WARREN: Everywhere along the front the color-bearers and officers sprang out, and, without more firing, our men advanced, capturing all the enemy remaining. During this last charge my horse was fatally shot within a few paces of the line where the enemy made his last stand, an orderly by my side was killed, and Colonel Richardson, of the 7th Wisconsin, who sprang between me and the enemy, was severely wounded.[8]

⏤ JOHN KELLOGG: We then drove them from their works across an open field, pursuing them closely about three-quarters of a mile, taking many prisoners and killing and wounding many of the enemy.[9]

— Philip Cheek: At dark, we were the victors at the battle of Five Forks, gaining the honor of capturing Pickett's Division.[10]

— George Pickett: Our loss in killed and wounded was very severe, and a good many were captured.[11]

— Horace Porter: As I galloped past a group of men on the Boydton plank-road, my orderly called out to them the news of the victory. The only response he got was from one of them, who raised his open hand to his face, put his thumb to his nose, and yelled: "No, you don't— April fool!"[12]

— Robert E. Lee: I see no prospect of doing more than holding our position here till night. I am not certain that I can do that. . . . The brigades on Hatcher's Run are cut off from us; enemy have broken through our lines and intercepted between us and them. . . . I advise that all preparation be made for leaving Richmond tonight.[13]

— George Alfred Townsend: The scene at Gravelly Run meeting-house at 8 and at 10 o'clock on Saturday night, is one of the solemn contrasts of the war, and, I hope, the last of them. A little frame church, planted among the pines, and painted white, with cool, green window-shutters, holds at its foot a gallery for the negroes, and at the head a varnished pulpit. I found its pews moved to the green plain over the threshold, and on its bare floors the screaming wounded. Blood ran in little rills across the planks, and human feet treading in them had made indelible prints in every direction; the pulpit-lamps were doing duty, not to shed holy light upon holy pages, but to show the pale and dusty faces of the beseeching; and as they moved in and out, the groans and curses of the suffering replaced the gush of peaceful hymns and the deep responses to the preacher's prayers. Federal and Confederate lay together, the bitterness of noon assuaged in the common tribulation of the night, and all the while came in the dripping stretchers, to place in this Golgotha new recruits for death and sorrow.[14]

— W. GORDON McCABE (*speaking of young Willie Pegram, the Boy Colonel, called Specs by his friends*): I had given him morphine in small quantities until he was easier, and he soon fell into a doze. . . . I shall never forget that night of waiting. I could only pray. He breathed heavily through the night, and passed into a stupor. I bound his wounds as well as I knew how and moistened his lips with water. Sunday morning he died as gently as possible.[15]

— SYLVANUS CADWALLADER: Reaching the City Point landing between sundown and dark, Mr. Lincoln (who had been notified of my coming by telegraph) sent his tug to the shore, and on its return met me at the hatchway of the lower deck with a beaming countenance and outstretched arms. As soon as I could convey my orders, he seized the flags, unfurled them one by one, and burst out: "Here is something material—something I can see, feel, and understand. This means victory. This *is* victory."[16]

— ULYSSES S. GRANT: I have ordered a general assault along the lines.[17]

— DAVID CARDWELL: Now begins the story of the retreat of Lee's army, when we fought daily, sometimes four or five times a day, till we reached Appomattox. But I leave that to any other man who craves the job.[18]

— GEORGE PICKETT: Lee's surrender is imminent. It is finished.[19]

— KARL MARX: The Confederacy seems to be at an end.[20]

— ROBERT E. LEE: —just as I have expected it would end from the first.[21]

— GEORGE PICKETT: Peace is born.[22]

W<small>E GO TO</small> C<small>HARLESTON</small> for our honeymoon, that city of old brick and ethereal black ironwork—and more beautiful women than I've ever seen in one place before. If Richmond was the capital of the Confederacy, Charleston was its heart: Calhoun the Nullifier . . . and a long line of fire-eaters later, Edmund Ruffin lit off the first cannon before the Federal resupply ships could reach the beleaguered garrison at Fort Sumter. (Four years later, just days after Lee's surrender at Appomattox, Edmund Ruffin shot himself—becoming, like Abe Lincoln and so many others, one more casualty of the war.)

Late Sunday morning I drive out to see Fort Moultrie—past azalea and wisteria in bloom, past Krispy Kreme, America's Favorite Doughnuts—where one soft April morning like this in the last century thousands of shots were fired "to reduce" Fort Sumter, as they used to say in those days. It's a slightly rainy day and I look out over the parapet toward Fort Sumter, a low-lying man-made island in the middle of the channel. At dawn, with rose-gold light gracing the clouds and the sand, peace and quiet erupted into a hell that would last four interminable years.

It's vacation, so I've lost track of the date, but in fact this rainy Sunday is the anniversary of the opening bombardment, and there's an encampment of Confederate reenactors set up beside the fort. (I have a brief but vivid fantasy of white men and Asians sitting around a similar scene, years hence—hooches and concertina wire—reenacting the war in Vietnam.) On this drizzly morning the reenactors are sitting around straw-covered dirt, underneath the kitchen tarp, talking low and slow—much as they probably would have been doing a lot of rainy time during the war: " . . . and not a dang thing anyone can do about it anyhow" drifts by me in a Southern cadence that I find soporific—while the mourning doves' lament breaks the hot stillness of the day. It seems like a long drive back to Charleston and the high-ceilinged antebellum room with full-length windows—shutters closed, already in April, against the heat of the day—and a floor of wide pine planks worn smooth by centuries of bare feet. . . .

Later that afternoon, after the rain has stopped and the sun has come out, we go to see Calhoun's grave, down by the marketplace. But it's

Sunday and the cemetery is chained and locked, so all we can do is look through the gate at the large tombstone with CALHOUN written on it, obscured by a huge magnolia and an equally huge live oak bending low over the grave.

We drive to the Calhoun monument near the center of town, past decaying buildings and the College of Charleston with its well-scrubbed white kids. Calhoun stands on his pillar in Marion Park, one arm akimbo, looking out over the roofs of lower Charleston toward Battery Park and the bay. Far beneath him, people down on their luck sit on the benches amidst worn grass and dirt, across the street from the Knights of Columbus and the Soft Rock Café. On the pedestal below Calhoun's pillar is written

> TRUTH JUSTICE
> and the
> CONSTITUTION

I've been reading Whitman's *Specimen Days*, and all day long his sentences have been going through my head:

> I have seen Calhoun's monument. . . . It is the desolated, ruined south; nearly the whole generation of young men between seventeen and thirty destroyed or maim'd; all the old families used up—the rich impoverish'd, the plantations covered with weeds . . . all that is Calhoun's real monument.[23]

At an antique store downtown we find an antebellum print of Calhoun, a silhouette of the man looking out over a palmettoed landscape from a window with venetian blinds, at the height of his power and prestige, the peak of his self-confidence or arrogance (it depended, no doubt, on your point of view). I tell the aging couple who own the store—they live in the small apartment upstairs, they inform us, third generation in the antique trade—that it captures the essence of the man. "A few years back they used to talk about pulling him down off his monument and putting Martin Luther King up there," the woman says. "Would've been another War."

The next day at breakfast, we read in the morning paper how a homeowner shot and killed a man running away from an attempted break-in. Elsewhere, this might be considered murder. But the county sheriff is quoted as saying, "I don't anticipate the Sheriff's Department will make charges." On the back page, where the rest of the story is buried, I read that the man killed was black, the shooter white. A city councilman says, "It's open season on black men."

Notes

CHAPTER 1

1. Robert Penn Warren, *The Legacy of the Civil War: Meditations on the Centennial* (New York: Random House, 1961), 81.
2. Edmund Wilson, *Patriotic Gore: Studies in the Literature of the American Civil War* (1962; reprint, foreword by C. Vann Woodward, Boston: Northeastern University Press, 1984), xiii–xiv.
3. Walt Whitman, *Walt Whitman's Civil War: Compiled and Edited from Published and Unpublished Sources by Walter Lowenfels, with the Assistance of Nan Braymer* (New York: Knopf, 1961), 3.
4. Ibid., 14.
5. Associated Press dispatch, quoted in Elijah Avey, *The Capture and Execution of John Brown* (1906; reprint, Chicago: Afro-Am Press, 1969), 69–70.
6. Walt Whitman, diary entry, December 26, 1864, quoted in Whitman, *Memoranda during the War [and] Death of Abraham Lincoln* (1875; reprint, edited by Roy P. Basler, Bloomington: Indiana University Press, 1962), 17.
7. Whitman to James Redpath, October 21, 1864, in Whitman, *Walt Whitman's Civil War*, 10–11.
8. Edmund N. Hatcher, ed., *The Last Four Weeks of the War* (Columbus, Ohio: Co-operative Publishing, 1892), iv. This book contains unattributed extracts from various Northern and Southern newspapers.
9. Mary Chesnut, *The Private Mary Chesnut: The Unpublished Civil War Diaries*, edited by C. Vann Woodward and Elisabeth Muhlenfeld (New York: Oxford University Press, 1984), 4–5.
10. Whitman, *Walt Whitman's Civil War*, 16–17.
11. Walt Whitman, "Origins of Attempted Secession," in *Specimen Days and Collect* (1882–83; reprint, New York: Dover Publications, 1995), 260–61.

12. Walt Whitman, "The Real War Will Never Get in the Books," in *Specimen Days*, 80–81.

13. Ibid, 81.

CHAPTER 2

1. Mary Chesnut, *Mary Chesnut's Civil War*, edited by C. Vann Woodward (New Haven: Yale University Press, 1981), 370. This was originally published in 1905 as *A Diary from Dixie*.

2. G. Moxley Sorrel, *Recollections of a Confederate Staff Officer* (1905; reprint, of 1959 ed., edited by Bell Irvin Wiley, Wilmington, N.C.: Broadfoot Publishing, 1987), 132.

3. Ulysses S. Grant, *Personal Memoirs of U. S. Grant* (New York: Charles L. Webster, 1885–86), 2:177–85.

4. C[harles] C. Coffin, "Late Scenes in Richmond," *Atlantic Monthly* 15 (June 1865): 748–49.

5. Chesnut, *Mary Chesnut's Civil War*, 607.

6. Walt Whitman, "A Night Battle, over a Week Since," in *Specimen Days*, 35.

7. Rufus R. Dawes to his wife, May 3–September 1, 1864, in *Service with the Sixth Wisconsin Volunteers* (1890; reprint, Dayton, Ohio: Morningside Bookshop, 1984), 249–99.

8. Alexander Gardner, *Gardner's Photographic Sketch Book of the War*, 2 vols. (1866; reprint, 2 vols. in 1, introduction by E. F. Bleiler, New York: Dover Publications, 1959), commentary to plates 77 and 83.

9. Chesnut, *Mary Chesnut's Civil War*, 114.

10. William Clark Corson to Jennie Hill Caldwell, July 11, 1864, in Corson, *My Dear Jennie: A Collection of Love Letters from a Confederate Soldier to his Fiancée during the Period 1861–1865*, edited by Blake W. Corson (Richmond, Va.: Dietz Press, 1982), 119–20.

11. Unknown to Constance Cary Harrison, quoted in Mrs. Burton [Constance Cary] Harrison, *Recollections, Grave and Gay* (New York: Scribner's, 1911), 151.

12. Dr. Henry Alexander White quoted in John B. Gordon, *Reminiscences of the Civil War* (1904; reprint, Dayton, Ohio: Morningside Bookshop, 1985), 419.

13. John Gibbon, *Personal Recollections of the Civil War* (1928; reprint, introduction by Don Russell, Dayton, Ohio: Morningside Bookshop, 1978), 291.

14. Ward Hill Lamon, *Recollections of Abraham Lincoln, 1847–1865* (Chicago: A. C. McClurg, 1895), 115–16 (quotation).

15. Grant, *Personal Memoirs*, 2:424.

16. Andrew A. Humphreys, *The Virginia Campaign of '64 and '65* (1883; reprint, introduction by Chris Calkins, Wilmington, N.C.: Broadfoot Publishing, 1989), 327.

17. Grant, *Personal Memoirs*, 2:439.

18. Coffin, "Late Scenes," 749–50.

19. Horace Porter, *Campaigning with Grant*, (1897; reprint, [Alexandria, Va.]: Time-Life Books, 1981), 429 (quotation).

20. Philip Cheek and Mair Pointon, *History of the Sauk County Riflemen: Known as Company "A," Sixth Wisconsin Veteran Volunteer Infantry, 1861–1865* (1909; reprint, introduction by Alan T. Nolan, Gaithersburg, Md.: Butternut Press, 1984), 159.

21. Philip H. Sheridan to Ulysses S. Grant, March 31, 1865, in U.S. War Department, *The War of the Rebellion: A Compilation of the Official Records of the Union and Confederate Armies* (Washington, D.C.: U.S. Government Printing Office, 1880–1901), ser. 1, vol. 46, pt. 3, p. 380 (hereafter cited as *Official Records*).

22. Monthly record of current events, *Harper's New Monthly Magazine* 30 (May 1865): 802.

23. Grant, *Personal Memoirs*, 2:440.

24. Walt Whitman, "Hospitals Closing," in *Specimen Days*, 76.

25. Walter H. Taylor, *Four Years with General Lee* (1877; reprint, introduction by James I. Robertson, Jr., Bloomington: Indiana University Press, 1962), 149–50.

26. Morris Schaff, *The Sunset of the Confederacy* (1912; reprint, Gaithersburg, Md.: Butternut Press, 1986), 19.

27. Robert E. Lee to John C. Breckinridge, April 1, 1865, in *Official Records*, ser. 1, vol. 46, pt. 3, p. 1371.

28. Schaff, *Sunset*, 19–20.

29. Robert E. Lee [Jr.], *Recollections and Letters of General Robert E. Lee, by His Son* (New York: Doubleday, 1904), 147–48.

30. Thomas Taylor Munford, "Five Forks: The Waterloo of the Confederacy, or the Last Days of Fitz Lee's Cavalry Division" [typescript, ca. 1908], Mss5:1 M9237:1, Virginia Historical Society, Richmond, pp. 2–3.

31. Spencer Glasgow Welch to Cordelia Strother Welch, August 2, 1863, in Welch, *A Confederate Surgeon's Letters to His Wife* (1911; reprint, Marietta, Ga.: Continental Book Company, 1954), 68.

32. James Longstreet, *From Manassas to Appomattox: Memoirs of the Civil War in America* (1898; reprint, Secaucus, N.J.: Blue and Grey Press, 1985), 386–87.

33. George Pickett to LaSalle Corbell, July 3, 1863, in Pickett, *The Heart of a Soldier:*

As Revealed in the Intimate Letters of Genl. George E. Pickett, C.S.A., edited by LaSalle Corbell Pickett (New York: Seth Moyle, 1913), 94. Though it is currently thought that Pickett's widow at the very least significantly edited these letters (and may indeed have substantially fabricated them from other, more reliable sources), I have quoted from them because, in the end, there are few historical records—even supposed eyewitness accounts—that are, in the face of personal bias or subjectivity, or the mutability of memory, entirely accurate. These letters have, in any case, over time come to form a significant piece of the lore of the Lost Cause.

34. Pickett to LaSalle Corbell, July 4, 1863, in Pickett, *Heart*, 98 (quotation).
35. Pickett to LaSalle Corbell, July 3, 1863, in Pickett, *Heart*, 96.
36. Walter Harrison, *Pickett's Men: A Fragment of War History* (1870; reprint, introduction by Gary W. Gallagher, Gaithersburg, Md.: Butternut Press, 1984), 97.
37. Joshua Lawrence Chamberlain, *The Passing of the Armies: An Account of the Final Campaign of the Army of the Potomac, Based upon Personal Reminiscences of the Fifth Army Corps* (1915; reprint, Dayton, Ohio: Morningside Bookshop, 1982), 146.
38. Frank A. Haskell, *Haskell of Gettysburg: His Life and Civil War Papers*, edited by Frank L. Byrne and Andrew T. Weaver (1970; reprint, Kent, Ohio: Kent State University Press, 1989), 155.
39. Pickett to LaSalle Corbell, July 12, 1863, in Pickett, *Heart*, 107.
40. Robert E. Lee to Charlotte Lee, quoted in Clifford Dowdey, *Lee* (Boston: Little, Brown, 1965; reprint, Gettysburg, Pa.: Stan Clark Military Books, 1991), 394.
41. Sorrel, *Recollections*, 163.
42. Ibid., 48.
43. Haskell, *Haskell of Gettysburg*, 158.
44. Francis W. Dawson, *Reminiscences of Confederate Service, 1861–1865* (1882; reprint, edited by Bell I. Wiley, Baton Rouge: Louisiana State University Press, 1980), 97.

CHAPTER 3

1. *Confederate Veteran* 7 (1899): 187–88, 332–35, 572.
2. Charles K. Moser, "Introductory Note," May 5, 1943, to Munford, "Five Forks."
3. George E. Smith, "In the Ranks at Fredericksburg," pt. 1, in *Battles and Leaders of the Civil War: Being for the Most Part Contributions by Union and Confederate Officers, Based upon "The Century War Series,"* edited by R[obert] U. Johnson and C[larence] C. Buel (1884–88; reprint, introduction by Roy F. Nichols, New York: T. Yoseloff, 1956), 3:142. This was originally published in *Century Magazine* 33 (March 1887): 806.

4. George F. Root, *Battle Cry of Freedom* (Chicago: Root and Cady, 1862), adapted for the Confederacy by H. L. Schreiner (music) and W. H. Barnes (lyrics), in James M. McPherson, *Battle Cry of Freedom: The Civil War Era* (New York: Oxford University Press, 1988), vi.

5. Herbert C. Saunders, account of an interview with Robert E. Lee, November 1865, in R. E. Lee [Jr.], *Recollections and Letters*, 231–32.

6. W. Harrison, *Pickett's Men*, 9.

7. Thomas Jefferson, "Draft Declaration and Protest of the Commonwealth of Virginia, on the Principles of the Constitution of the United States of America, and on the Violations of them" [December 1825], in Jefferson, *Public and Private Papers* (New York: Vintage Books/Library of America, 1990), 156–58.

8. Robert E. Lee to C. Chauncey Barr, January 5, 1866, in R. E. Lee [Jr.], *Recollections and Letters*, 225.

9. Jeremiah Best, "Wall Street in War Time," *Harper's New Monthly Magazine* 30 (April 1865): 615–16.

10. Robert E. Lee to Jefferson Davis, April 1, 1865, in Lee, *Wartime Papers of Robert E. Lee*, edited by Clifford Dowdey and Louis H. Manarin (1961; reprint, New York: Da Capo Press, 1987), 922.

11. E.[dwin] P. Whipple, "The Causes of Foreign Enmity to the United States," *Atlantic Monthly* 15 (March 1865): 373–74.

12. E[dward] E[verett] Hale, "Edward Everett," *Atlantic Monthly* 15 (March 1865): 345.

13. Dr. Josiah C. Curtis, report to the American Medical Association, quoted in Avery Craven, *Civil War in the Making, 1815–1860* (Baton Rouge: Louisiana State University Press, 1959), 14.

14. Orestes A. Brownson, *The Laboring Classes (1840) with Brownson's Defence of the Article on the Laboring Classes* (reprint, introduction by Martin K. Doudna, Delmar, N.Y.: Scholars' Facsimiles and Reprints, 1978), 12.

15. Lydia Maria Child to William Cutler, July 10, 1862, in *". . . The Real War Will Never Get in the Books": Selections from Writers during the Civil War*, edited by Louis P. Masur (New York: Oxford University Press, 1993), 48.

16. Alexis de Tocqueville, *Democracy in America*, translated by Henry Reeve and Francis Bowen (1835–40; reprint, edited by Phillips Bradley, New York: Knopf, 1945), 1:418.

17. *Columbus (Georgia) Sentinel*, January 23, 1851, quoted in Craven, *Civil War*, 88.

18. John C. Calhoun, speech on the reception of abolition petitions, U.S. Senate, February 6, 1837, in *Slavery Defended: The Views of the Old South*, edited by Eric

L. McKitrick (Englewood Cliffs, N.J.: Prentice-Hall, 1963), 12–14.

19. William H. Seward, *The Irrepressible Conflict: A Speech Delivered at Rochester, Monday, Oct. 25, 1858* (New York: Tribune Office, [1860]), 3.

20. [Schuyler Colfax et al.], *The Border Ruffian Code in Kansas* (New York: Tribune Office, [1856]), 1.

21. Abraham Lincoln, speech at the fourth Lincoln-Douglas Debate, Charlestown, Illinois, September 18, 1858, in Lincoln, *The Essential Abraham Lincoln*, edited by John Gabriel Hunt (New York: Gramercy Books, 1993), 153.

22. Monthly record of current events, *Harper's New Monthly Magazine* 26 (January 1863): 267.

23. Charles O'Conor, "The Real Question Stated, Letter to a Committee of Merchants, Dec. 20, 1859," appended to Seward, *Irrepressible Conflict*, 14.

24. A Peaceable Man [Nathaniel Hawthorne], "Chiefly about War-Matters," in " . . . The Real War," edited by Masur, 173 (first published in *Atlantic Monthly* 10 [July 1862]: 43–61).

25. Chesnut, *Mary Chesnut's Civil War*, 29.

26. Fitz-Hugh Ludlow, "If Massa Put Guns into Our Han's," *Atlantic Monthly* 15 (April 1865): 504–8.

27. James Henry Hammond to James Henry "Harry" Hammond, February 19, 1856, in Lewis Simpson, *The Fable of the Southern Writer* (Baton Rouge: Louisiana State University Press, 1994), 41.

28. Karl Marx, "The Civil War in the United States," *Die Presse* (Vienna), November 7, 1861, in Karl Marx and Friedrich Engels, *The Civil War in the United States*, Centennial [3d] ed. (New York: International Publishers, 1961), 81.

29. James H. Thornwell, quoted without citation in Craven, *Civil War*, 102.

30. Frederick Law Olmsted, *A Journey in the Back Country* (1860; reprint, New York: B. Franklin, 1970), 443–44.

31. William Ellery Channing quoted in Theodore D. Weld, *American Slavery as It Is: Testimony of a Thousand Witnesses* (1839), in *Slavery Attacked: The Abolitionist Crusade*, edited by John L. Thomas (Englewood Cliffs, N.J.: Prentice-Hall, 1965), 61–62.

32. Judge Nichols of Kentucky, speech, 1837, quoted in Olmsted, *Journey*, 300n.

33. Tocqueville, *Democracy*, 1:411.

34. John Sergeant Wise, *The End of an Era* (1899; reprint, edited by Curtis Carroll Davis, New York: T. Yoseloff, 1965), 82.

35. "The Richmond Black Code" (1859), in *A Richmond Reader, 1733–1983*, edited by

Maurice Duke and Daniel Jordan, introduction by Louis D. Rubin Jr. (Chapel Hill: University of North Carolina Press, 1983), 110.

36. Frederick Douglass, *Narrative of the Life of Frederick Douglass: An American Slave* (1845; New York: New American Library, 1968), 92–93.

37. Olmsted, *Journey*, 476.

38. Douglass, *Narrative*, 76.

39. Avey, *Capture and Execution*, 30.

40. John Brown, address to the court, quoted in Avey, *Capture and Execution*, 25.

41. C[lement] L. Vallandigham quoted in Avey, *Capture and Execution*, 132.

42. Richard Taylor, *Destruction and Reconstruction: Personal Experiences of the Late War* (1879; reprint, edited by Richard B. Harwell, New York: Longmans, Green, 1955), 311.

43. Coffin, "Late Scenes," 746.

44. Peter Randolph, "From Slave Cabin to the Pulpit" (1893), in *A Richmond Reader*, edited by Duke and Jordan, 135–36.

45. Ralph Waldo Emerson, journal entry, 1844, quoted in Lewis Simpson, *Mind and the American Civil War: A Meditation on Lost Causes* (Baton Rouge: Louisiana State University Press, 1989), 57.

46. Tocqueville, *Democracy*, 1:373, 390.

CHAPTER 4

1. J[ohn] B. Jones, *A Rebel War Clerk's Diary at the Confederate States Capital* (1866; reprint, [Alexandria, Va.]: Time-Life Books, 1982), 2:464.

2. Bushrod R. Johnson, report of April 10, 1865, in *Official Records*, ser. 1, vol. 46, pt. 1, p. 1288.

3. Chamberlain, *Passing*, 173n.

4. Thomas Rosser quoted in Munford, "Five Forks," 39.

5. Thomas T. Munford, testimony, in U.S. Army, *Proceedings, Findings, and Opinions of the Court Of Inquiry: Convened by Order of the President of the United States . . . in the Case of Gouverneur K. Warren* (Washington, D.C.: U.S. Government Printing Office, 1883), 1:444.

6. Jefferson Davis to Thomas T. Munford, May 28, 1889, quoted in Munford, "Five Forks," 44.

7. Humphreys, *Virginia Campaign*, 349n.

8. Robert E. Lee to Jefferson Davis, April 20, 1865, in Lee, *Wartime Papers*, 939.

9. Spencer Glasgow Welch to Cordelia Strother Welch, October 2, 1864, in Welch, *Confederate Surgeon's Letters*, 107.

10. Jennie Hill Caldwell to William Clark Corson, March 8, 1865, in Corson, *My Dear Jennie*, 141.

11. Hatcher, *Last Four Weeks*, 98.

12. Ibid., 101.

13. Gordon, *Reminiscences*, 374–75.

14. William Clark Corson to Jennie Hill Caldwell, January 17, 1865, in Corson, *My Dear Jennie*, 134–35.

15. David Cardwell, "The Battle of Five Forks," *Confederate Veteran* 22 (March 1914): 117.

16. Coffin, "Late Scenes," 750–51.

17. Ulysses S. Grant to Abraham Lincoln, April 1, 1865, in *Official Records*, ser. 1, vol. 46, pt. 3, p. 393.

18. Gouverneur K. Warren to Alexander Webb, March 31, 1865, in *Official Records*, ser. 1, vol. 46, pt. 3, p. 366.

19. George G. Meade to Gouverneur K. Warren, March 31, 1865, in *Official Records*, ser. 1, vol. 46, pt. 3, p. 367.

20. Gouverneur K. Warren to George Meade, March 31, 1865, in *Official Records*, ser. 1, vol. 46, pt. 3, p. 367.

21. Grant, *Personal Memoirs*, 2:266.

22. Gouverneur K. Warren, *An Account of the Operations of the Fifth Army Corps at the Battle of Five Forks* (New York: William M. Franklin, 1866), 31.

23. Grant, *Personal Memoirs*, 2:444.

24. Philip Sheridan, report of May 16, 1865, in *Official Records*, ser. 1, vol. 46, pt. 1, p. 1105.

25. Warren, *Account*, 5.

26. Chamberlain, *Passing*, 122.

27. Porter, *Campaigning*, 436.

28. Philip Sheridan, report of April 2, 1865, in *Official Records*, ser. 1, vol. 46, pt. 1, p. 1100.

29. Robert E. Lee, report of April 1, 1865, in *Official Records*, ser. 1, vol. 46, pt. 1, p. 1264.

30. Philip Sheridan, report of May 16, 1865, in *Official Records*, ser. 1, vol. 46, pt. 1, p. 1105.

31. Chamberlain, *Passing*, 151.

32. Gouverneur K. Warren to Emily Warren, July 13, 1872, in *Battles and Leaders of the Civil War*, edited by Johnson and Buel, 3:307–9n.

33. Porter, *Campaigning*, 435–36.

34. J[ohn] C. Goolsby, "Crenshaw Battery, Pegram's Battalion, Confederate States Artillery," *Southern Historical Society Papers* 28 (1900): 371.

35. Munford, "Five Forks," 27–28.

36. W. Harrison, *Pickett's Men*, 139.

37. Samuel Crawford, report of April 20, 1865, in *Official Records*, ser. 1, vol. 46, pt. 1, p. 880.

38. Fitzhugh Lee, report of April 22, 1865, in *Official Records*, ser. 1, vol. 46, pt. 1, p. 1299.

39. U.S. Army, *Proceedings*, 1:447. Successive quotes are from the same source, 447–48.

40. William T. Sherman to Henry W. Halleck, September 17, 1863, in *Official Records*, ser. 1, vol. 30, pt. 3, p. 696.

41. Joseph Roberts, *Handbook of Artillery* (1863), 50–51, quoted in Jay Luvaas and Harold W. Nelson, eds., *The U.S. Army War College Guide to the Battle of Gettysburg* (New York: Harper and Row, 1986), 209.

42. Thomas Mellon to James Mellon, quoted in Matthew Josephson, *The Robber Barons: The Great American Capitalists, 1861–1901* (1934; New York: Harcourt Brace Jovanovich, 1962), 50.

43. John S. Schooley, "The Petroleum Region of America," *Harper's New Monthly Magazine* 30 (April 1865): 563.

44. Charlotte Forten [Grimké], journal entry, January 24, 1863, in *Black Writers and the American Civil War*, edited by Richard A. Long (Secaucus, N.J.: Blue and Grey Press, 1988), 178.

45. Anonymous to Jefferson Davis, January 11, 1863, quoted in Allen Tate, *Jefferson Davis: His Rise and Fall, a Biographical Narrative* (New York: Minton, Balch, 1929), 237.

46. Thomas Wentworth Higginson, *Army Life in a Black Regiment* (1870; reprint, [Alexandria, Va.]: Time-Life Books, 1982), 47–48.

47. Hatcher, *Last Four Weeks*, 97.

48. George Pickett, report to Robert E. Lee, in W. Harrison, *Pickett's Men*, 146.

49. Munford, "Five Forks," 29–30.

50. Pickett to LaSalle Corbell Pickett, April 2, 1865, in Pickett, *Heart*, 174–75.

51. Cordelia Strother Welch to Georgia Strother, March 1865, in Welch, *Confederate Surgeon's Letters*, 125–26.

52. Chesnut, *Mary Chesnut's Civil War*, 737.

53. Pickett to LaSalle Corbell Pickett, June 3, 1864, in Pickett, *Heart*, 133.

54. Unknown to Joshua Lawrence Chamberlain, in Willard M. Wallace, *Soul of the Lion: A Biography of Joshua L. Chamberlain* (New York: Thomas Nelson, 1960), 99.

CHAPTER 5

1. Coffin, "Late Scenes," 751.

2. Hatcher, *Last Four Weeks*, 94.

3. George Alfred Townsend, *Campaigns of a Non-Combatant* (1866; reprint, [Alexandria, Va.]: Time-Life Books, 1982), 324.

4. Gouverneur K. Warren, report of December 1, 1865, in *Official Records*, ser. 1, vol. 46, pt. 1, p. 835.

5. Pickett to LaSalle Corbell Pickett, April 2, 1865, in Pickett, *Heart*, 174.

6. Coffin, "Late Scenes," 751.

7. Pickett to LaSalle Corbell Pickett, April 2, 1865, in Pickett, *Heart*, 173.

8. Gouverneur K. Warren, report of December 1, 1865, in *Official Records*, ser. 1, vol. 46, pt. 1, p. 835.

9. John A. Kellogg, report of April 10, 1865, in *Official Records*, ser. 1, vol. 46, pt. 1, pp. 885–86.

10. Cheek and Pointon, *History*, 164.

11. George Pickett, report to Robert E. Lee, in W. Harrison, *Pickett's Men*, 148.

12. Porter, *Campaigning*, 442.

13. Robert E. Lee to John C. Breckinridge, April 2, 1865, *Official Records*, ser. 1, vol. 46, pt. 1, p. 1264.

14. Townsend, *Campaigns*, 327–28.

15. W. Gordon McCabe quoted in Douglas Southall Freeman, *Lee's Lieutenants* (New York: Scribner's, 1944–46), 3:673–74.

16. Sylvanus Cadwallader, *Three Years with Grant: As Recalled by War Correspondent Sylvanus Cadwallader*, edited by Benjamin Thomas (New York: Knopf, 1956), 307.

17. Porter, *Campaigning*, 443.

18. Cardwell, "Battle," 117–120.

19. Pickett to LaSalle Corbell Pickett, April 9, 1865, in Pickett, *Heart*, 176.

20. Karl Marx to Friedrich Engels, March 4, 1865, in Marx and Engels, *Civil War*, 274.

21. Wise, *End of an Era*, 429.

22. Pickett to LaSalle Corbell Pickett, April 9, 1865, in Pickett, *Heart*, 179.

23. Walt Whitman, "Calhoun's Real Monument," in *Specimen Days*, 76.

Sources

Avey, Elijah. *The Capture and Execution of John Brown.* 1906. Reprint, Chicago: Afro-Am Press, 1969.

Bearss, Ed[win C.], and Chris Calkins. *Battle of Five Forks.* Virginia Civil War Battles and Leaders Series. Lynchburg, Va.: H. E. Howard, 1985.

Best, Jeremiah. "Wall Street in War Time." *Harper's New Monthly Magazine* 30 (April 1865): 615–23.

Brownson, Orestes A. *The Laboring Classes (1840) with Brownson's Defence of the Article on the Laboring Classes.* Reprint, introduction by Martin K. Doudna, Delmar, N.Y.: Scholars' Facsimiles and Reprints, 1978.

Cadwallader, Sylvanus. *Three Years with Grant: As Recalled by War Correspondent Sylvanus Cadwallader.* Edited by Benjamin P. Thomas. New York: Knopf, 1956.

Cardwell, David. "The Battle of Five Forks." *Confederate Veteran* 22 (March 1914): 117–20.

Chamberlain, Joshua Lawrence. *The Passing of the Armies: An Account of the Final Campaign of the Army of the Potomac, Based upon Personal Reminiscences of the Fifth Army Corps.* 1915. Reprint, Dayton, Ohio: Morningside Bookshop, 1982.

Cheek, Philip, and Mair Pointon. *History of the Sauk County Riflemen: Known as Company "A," Sixth Wisconsin Veteran Volunteer Infantry, 1861–1865.* 1909. Reprint, introduction by Alan T. Nolan, Gaithersburg, Md.: Butternut Press, 1984.

Chesnut, Mary. *Mary Chesnut's Civil War.* 1905. Reprint, edited by C. Vann Woodward, New Haven: Yale University Press, 1981.

———. *The Private Mary Chesnut: The Unpublished Civil War Diaries.* Edited by C. Vann Woodward and Elisabeth Muhlenfeld. New York: Oxford University Press, 1984.

Coffin, C[harles] C. "Late Scenes in Richmond." *Atlantic Monthly* 15 (June 1865): 744–55.

[Colfax, Schuyler, et al.] *The Border Ruffian Code in Kansas.* New York: Tribune Office, [1856].

Corson, William Clark. *My Dear Jennie: A Collection of Love Letters from a Confederate Soldier to his Fiancée during the Period 1861–1865*. Edited by Blake W. Corson. Richmond, Va.: Dietz Press, 1982.

Craven, Avery. *Civil War in the Making, 1815–1860*. Baton Rouge: Louisiana State University Press, 1959.

Dawes, Rufus R. *Service with the Sixth Wisconsin Volunteers*. 1890. Reprint, Dayton, Ohio: Morningside Bookshop, 1984.

Dawson, Francis W. *Reminiscences of Confederate Service, 1861–1865*. 1882. Reprint, edited by Bell I. Wiley, Baton Rouge: Louisiana State University Press, 1980.

Douglass, Frederick. *Narrative of the Life of Frederick Douglass: An American Slave*. 1845; New York: New American Library, 1968.

Dowdey, Clifford. *Lee*. 1965. Reprint, Gettysburg, Pa.: Stan Clark Military Books, 1991.

Duke, Maurice, and Daniel P. Jordan, eds. *A Richmond Reader, 1733–1983*. Introduction by Louis D. Rubin Jr. Chapel Hill: University of North Carolina Press, 1983.

Freeman, Douglas Southall. *Lee's Lieutenants*. 3 vols. New York: Scribner's, 1944–46.

Gardner, Alexander. *Gardner's Photographic Sketch Book of the War*. 2 vols. 1866. Reprint (2 vols. in 1), introduction by E. F. Bleiler, New York: Dover Publications, 1959.

Gibbon, John. *Personal Recollections of the Civil War*. 1928. Reprint, introduction by Don Russell, Dayton, Ohio: Morningside Bookshop, 1978.

Goolsby, J[ohn] C. "Crenshaw Battery, Pegram's Battalion, Confederate States Artillery." *Southern Historical Society Papers* 28 (1900): 336–76.

Gordon, John B. *Reminiscences of the Civil War*. 1904. Reprint, Dayton, Ohio: Morningside Bookshop, 1985.

Grant, Ulysses S. *Personal Memoirs of U. S. Grant*. 2 vols. New York: Charles L. Webster, 1885–86.

Hale, E[dward] E. "Edward Everett." *Atlantic Monthly* 15 (March 1865): 342–49.

Harrison, Mrs. Burton [Constance Cary]. *Recollections, Grave and Gay*. New York: Scribner's, 1911.

Harrison, Walter. *Pickett's Men: A Fragment of War History*. 1870. Reprint, introduction by Gary W. Gallagher, Gaithersburg, Md.: Butternut Press, 1984.

Haskell, Frank A. *Haskell of Gettysburg: His Life and Civil War Papers*. Edited by Frank L. Byrne and Andrew T. Weaver. 1970. Reprint, Kent, Ohio: Kent State University Press, 1989.

Hatcher, Edmund N., ed. *The Last Four Weeks of the War*. Columbus, Ohio: Co-operative Publishing, 1892.

Higginson, Thomas Wentworth. *Army Life in a Black Regiment* 1870. Reprint, [Alexandria, Va.]: Time-Life Books, 1982.

Humphreys, Andrew A. *The Virginia Campaign of '64 and '65: The Army of the Potomac and the Army of the James.* 1883. Reprint, introduction by Chris Calkins, Wilmington, N.C.: Broadfoot Publishing, 1989.

Jefferson, Thomas. *Public and Private Papers.* New York: Vintage Books/Library of America, 1990.

Johnson, R[obert] U., and C[larence] C. Buel, eds. *Battles and Leaders of the Civil War: Being for the Most Part Contributions by Union and Confederate Officers, Based upon "The Century War Series."* 4 vols. 1884–87. Reprint, introduction by Roy F. Nichols, New York: T. Yoseloff, 1956.

Jones, J[ohn] B. *A Rebel War Clerk's Diary at the Confederate States Capital.* 2 vols.1866. Reprint, [Alexandria, Va.]: Time-Life Books, 1982.

Josephson, Matthew. *The Robber Barons: The Great American Capitalists, 1861–1901.* 1934. New York: Harcourt Brace Jovanovich, 1962.

Lamon, Ward Hill. *Recollections of Abraham Lincoln, 1847–1865.* Chicago: A. C. McClurg, 1895.

Lee, Robert E. *Wartime Papers of Robert E. Lee.* Edited by Clifford Dowdey and Louis H. Manarin. 1961. Reprint, New York: Da Capo Press, 1987.

Lee, Robert E., [Jr.]. *Recollections and Letters of General Robert E. Lee, by His Son.* New York: Doubleday, 1904.

Lincoln, Abraham. *The Essential Abraham Lincoln.* Edited by John Gabriel Hunt. New York: Gramercy Books, 1993.

Long, Richard A., ed. *Black Writers and the American Civil War.* Secaucus, N.J.: Blue and Grey Press, 1988.

Longstreet, James. *From Manassas to Appomattox: Memoirs of the Civil War in America.* 1898. Reprint, Secaucus, N.J.: Blue and Grey Press, 1985.

Ludlow, Fitz-Hugh. "If Massa Put Guns into Our Han's." *Atlantic Monthly* 15 (April 1865): 504–12.

Luvaas, Jay, and Harold W. Nelson, eds. *The U.S. Army War College Guide to the Battle of Gettysburg.* New York: Harper and Row, 1986.

Marx, Karl, and Friedrich Engels. *The Civil War in the United States.* Centennial [3d] ed. New York: International Publishers, 1961.

Masur, Louis P., ed. *". . . The Real War Will Never Get in the Books": Selections from Writers during the Civil War.* New York: Oxford University Press, 1993.

McKitrick, Eric L., ed. *Slavery Defended: The Views of the Old South.* Englewood Cliffs, N.J.: Prentice-Hall, 1963.

McPherson, James M. *Battle Cry of Freedom: The Civil War Era.* New York: Oxford University Press, 1988.

Munford, Thomas Taylor. "Five Forks: The Waterloo of the Confederacy, or the Last Days of Fitz Lee's Cavalry Division" [typescript, ca. 1908]. Mss5:1 M9237:1, Virginia Historical Society, Richmond.

Olmsted, Frederick Law. *A Journey in the Back Country*. 1860. Reprint, New York: B. Franklin, 1970.

Pickett, George E. *The Heart of a Soldier: As Revealed in the Intimate Letters of Genl. George E. Pickett, C.S.A.* Edited by LaSalle Corbell Pickett. New York: Seth Moyle, 1913.

Porter, Horace. *Campaigning with Grant*. 1897. Reprint, [Alexandria, Va.]: Time-Life Books, 1981.

Schaff, Morris. *The Sunset of the Confederacy*. 1912. Reprint, Gaithersburg, Md.: Butternut Press, 1986.

Schooley, John S. "The Petroleum Region of America." *Harper's New Monthly Magazine* 30 (April 1865): 562–74.

Seward, William H. *The Irrepressible Conflict: A Speech Delivered at Rochester, Monday, Oct. 25, 1858*. New York: Tribune Office, [1860].

Simpson, Lewis P. *The Fable of the Southern Writer*. Baton Rouge: Louisiana State University Press, 1994.

———. *Mind and the American Civil War: A Meditation on Lost Causes*. Baton Rouge: Louisiana State University Press, 1989.

Sorrel, G. Moxley. *Recollections of a Confederate Staff Officer*. 1905. Reprint of 1959 ed., edited by Bell Irvin Wiley, Wilmington, N.C.: Broadfoot Publishing, 1987.

Tate, Allen. *Jefferson Davis: His Rise and Fall, a Biographical Narrative*. New York: Minton, Balch, 1929.

Taylor, Richard. *Destruction and Reconstruction: Personal Experiences of the Late War*. 1879. Reprint, edited by Richard B. Harwell, New York: Longmans, Green, 1955.

Taylor, Walter H. *Four Years with General Lee*. 1877. Reprint, introduction by James I. Robertson, Bloomington: Indiana University Press, 1962.

Thomas, John L., ed. *Slavery Attacked: The Abolitionist Crusade*. Englewood Cliffs, N.J.: Prentice-Hall, 1965.

Tocqueville, Alexis de. *Democracy in America*. Translated by Henry Reeve and Francis Bowen. 2 vols. 1835–40. Reprint, edited by Phillips Bradley, New York: Knopf, 1945.

Townsend, George Alfred. *Campaigns of a Non-Combatant*. 1866. Reprint, [Alexandria, Va.]: Time-Life Books, 1982.

U.S. Army. *Proceedings, Findings, and Opinions of the Court Of Inquiry: Convened by*

Order of the President of the United States . . . in the Case of Gouverneur K. Warren.
3 vols. Washington, D.C.: U.S. Government Printing Office, 1883.

U.S. War Department. *The War of the Rebellion: A Compilation of the Official Records of
the Union and Confederate Armies.* 128 vols. Washington, D.C.: U.S. Government
Printing Office, 1880–1901.

Wallace, Willard M. *Soul of the Lion: A Biography of Joshua L. Chamberlain.* New York:
Thomas Nelson, 1960.

Warren, Gouverneur K. *An Account of the Operations of the Fifth Army Corps at the
Battle of Five Forks, April 1, 1865, and the Battles and Movements Preliminary to It.*
New York: William M. Franklin, 1866.

Warren, Robert Penn. *The Legacy of the Civil War: Meditations on the Centennial.* New
York: Random House, 1961.

Welch, Spencer Glasgow. *A Confederate Surgeon's Letters to His Wife.* 1911. Reprint,
Marietta, Ga.: Continental Book Company, 1954.

Whipple, E[dwin] P. "The Causes of Foreign Enmity to the United States." *Atlantic
Monthly* 15 (March 1865): 372–76.

Whitman, Walt. *Memoranda during the War [and] Death of Abraham Lincoln.* 1875.
Reprint, edited with an introduction by Roy P. Basler, Bloomington: Indiana
University Press, 1962.

———. *Specimen Days and Collect.* 1882–83. Reprint, New York: Dover, 1995.

———. *Walt Whitman's Civil War: Compiled and Edited from Published and Unpublished
Sources by Walter Lowenfels, with the Assistance of Nan Braymer.* New York: Knopf,
1960.

Wilson, Edmund. *Patriotic Gore: Studies in the Literature of the American Civil War.*
1962. Reprint, foreword by C. Vann Woodward, Boston: Northeastern University
Press, 1984.

Wise, John Sergeant. *The End of an Era.* 1899. Reprint, edited and annotated by Curtis
Carroll Davis, New York: T. Yoseloff, 1965.

Acknowledgments

THOUGH WRITING IS A SOLITARY ART, a book depends for its life on the efforts of many individuals. My greatest debt of gratitude goes to Martha Bates, acquisitions editor at Michigan State University Press. After some two dozen other publishers had taken a pass on *Five Forks*, she saw enough value in it to share it with her colleagues and present it successfully to her editorial committee. Not least, she would always return my phone calls to discuss whatever obsessive detail I happened to be wondering about at any particular moment. I would also like to thank Sylvia Malik Robine, the marketing manager at MSU Press, for her enthusiastic support of my book, and Annette K. Tanner, the production manager, for her good cheer while dealing with the minutiae of computer files and photos.

My thanks also go to Louis Manarin, former Virginia state archivist, who at the start of my research shared his wisdom and knowledge with me and many years later was kind enough to review my manuscript and point out innumerable errors of fact and lore that I had let creep in. I am grateful as well to the various researchers and librarians, such as Warren Tsuneishi, former director of area studies at the Library of Congress, and others at the Virginia Historical Society in Richmond, and the Wisconsin Historical Society in Madison, who answered questions and offered facts and suggestions that helped me out. This list should also include Chris Calkins, historian at Petersburg National Battlefield, who (along with Ed Bearss) quite literally "wrote the book" on the Battle of Five Forks and who shared his knowledge with me. As a former English major, my training and expertise in historiography were sorely lacking, and I therefore have others to thank for whatever is scholarly or insightful in this book, though I take full responsibility for all errors and misstatements.

My thanks also to all the individuals who shared their time and support, including my close friends in Virginia, the late Peggy Hudgins and the late Dorothy Richardson, who opened their homes and hearts to me for many years. I owe a debt of gratitude as well to the many people who read and critiqued my manuscript at various stages of completion—not least Jim Harrison, who was kind enough to send my manuscript to Martha Bates, whom he knew as a skillful and innovative editor, along with a letter containing the encouraging sentiments he had expressed to me at several times when it seemed I might never find a publisher for this project.

Finally, I thank my wife, Katherine Mead, who held my hand through many years of whining and complaints, and—herself a writer—shared her thoughts and suggestions with me. Without her support and the support of all these other people, as well as that of unnamed friends and strangers and family members who offered wisdom or kindness when I most needed it (and put up for many years with my blabbering about the Civil War), it is doubtful that this book would ever have reached fruition.